ALL IN WITH THE ALMIGHTY

Parenting Special Needs Children by Faith

Elizabeth Newman

HGR EDITORIAL
Cover Concept by Sophia Newman
Graphic Design and Content Layout by Nathan Izzat

ISBN: 978-1-59684-979-2

NOTE: Words in boldface in Scripture passages represent the author's emphasis.

Quotations cited are for educational use.

Copyright © 2017 by Elizabeth Newman
Published by Derek Press
Cleveland, TN 37311
Printed in the United States of America

Dedication

To the One
who counts us all in the joy set before Him
and pours upon us abundant blessings
so that we may bless others.

Acknowledgments

My deepest thanks to those who contributed to, inspired, and supported this study:

My husband, Jody, and our daughters, Kate, Sophia, Gabriella, and Mia, my parents, Dr. James and Greta Kelso, my large and embracing family, Mia's devoted therapists and teachers, the Unlimited Ministry Team, Amy Heifner, Carmen Simons, Dara Fairgrieves, Homer Rhea, Jenine Newman, Jillian Palmiotto, Julie Gayler, Julie Spellissy, Karen Monette, Nathan Izzat, Pat Ritsema, Traci Abel, and each family sharing this special needs journey with me.

Contents

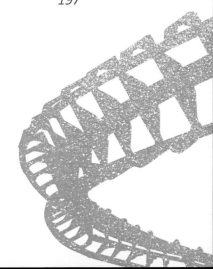

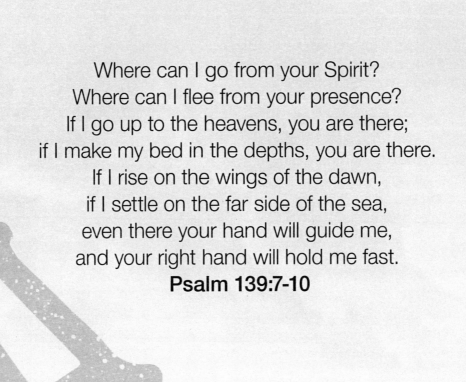

Where can I go from your Spirit?
Where can I flee from your presence?
If I go up to the heavens, you are there;
if I make my bed in the depths, you are there.
If I rise on the wings of the dawn,
if I settle on the far side of the sea,
even there your hand will guide me,
and your right hand will hold me fast.
Psalm 139:7-10

INTRODUCTION
GOD IS WITH US

ALWAYS AND EVERYWHERE

God promises there is no place too high or too low for His presence to abound. That's good news for all of us. It is particularly good news when we face overwhelming challenges, like caring for a child with special needs. Throughout this study, we are going to take a look at what God has to say personally, and collectively, about the significance of His presence in our lives. As we become more aware of His presence, we will explore how a relationship with God specifically impacts our perceptions and actions as we raise children with special needs.

I am sure you have all heard the analogy equating life to a roller coaster. Raising a child with daunting special needs gives a whole new meaning to that phrase. For me, life with my special needs daughter, Mia, translates to life on the infamous "giga-coaster" Kingda Ka. The Kingda Ka is dubbed a "giga-coaster" because, depending upon your perspective, it is one heck of a frightening, or an exhilarating, ride!

The Kingda Ka's speed, height, and drop top most other coasters in the United States. It reaches speeds of 128 miles per hour, takes riders 456 feet above the ground, and drops 418 feet straight down. The whole ride takes less than 30 seconds to experience, but when you are on it, it can feel like a lifetime. The cost to build such a ride comes close to $100 million! The Kingda Ka's perilous ride and enormous cost certainly equate to life with Mia for me.

To be honest, I have never been a fan of theme park roller coasters, and prior to Mia's arrival had never ridden one by choice. Yet, upon Mia's diagnosis, the roller coaster my life became is a ride unlike anything I could have imagined. And though I have been on this ride for many years, I have come to realize that no matter how long a parent has been raising a challenged child, we continue to spend hours in discussion and contemplation about this ride. We meditate, deliberate, and, at times, deteriorate over how high it will go, how fast, how big the drops will be, and how long this ride will last.

As we delve into God's Word, I invite you to go "all in with the Almighty" for our goal is to more fully experience His presence as we continually build a deeper daily relationship with Him. We need God with us every inch of this track to manage this ride with any semblance of grace. Over the next 11 Study Sessions, we will apply biblical truths as we explore what God's top 10 roller coaster riding tips might look like.

The list below captures the essence of God's message for me:

1. **Trust the Designer and Maintenance Man**
2. **Activate Your Spirit of Courage**
3. **Commit to Follow the Track**
4. **Experience the Freedom to Scream**
5. **Find Camaraderie with a Train Full of Riders**
6. **Display Compassion for Those in the Same Seat**
7. **Process the View Through God's Eyes**
8. **Let Go of the Handlebars**
9. **Recharge for the Ride**
10. **Focus on Home**

We will examine each of these 10 aspects of roller coaster riding under a scriptural microscope while engaging in the centuries-old practice of Christian fellowship. Acts 2:44-47 describes early Christian fellowship, particularly in the light of the persecution they faced, in the following ways. They . . .

- Met together with a common belief.
- Preached and studied Scripture.
- Encouraged each other to live in Christ Jesus.
- Honored the life and sacrifice of Christ Jesus.
- Prayed together.

Read the passage below for yourself:

> All the believers were together and had everything in common. They sold property
> and possessions to give to anyone who had need. Every day they continued to meet
> together in the temple courts. They broke bread in their homes and ate together with
> glad and sincere hearts praising God and enjoying the favor of all the people.
> And the Lord added to their number daily those who were being saved.
> **Acts 2:44-4**

As we follow the example of our Christian forefathers and come together to master the "special needs roller coaster," we will have the opportunity to spend individual time in Scripture study with the Lord. We will also meet periodically in small group gatherings to emphasize common beliefs as we study the message of Scripture and encourage each other in Christ. As praise and prayer are an integral part of Christian fellowships, each session will conclude with an opportunity to celebrate the gift of faith and lift up prayer petitions.

The study is designed to incorporate a minimum of 11 small group meetings, however, the questions in the 11 Discussion Group pages can be divided into smaller sets for more frequent meetings. This will allow your group to progress through this study at the rate which best accommodates the participants involved. Whether you work through these pages in 11 weeks, 11 months, or several years, God will provide just the message you need to hear at just the time you need to hear it. He is faithful to ensure His living Word bears fruit.

Individual reflection feeds and strengthens your personal relationship with Christ; however, with all the additional parenting pressures moms and dads of special needs children face, quiet time can be in short supply. As you approach each section's reading, ask the Lord to give you the time He knows you need, and then do as much of the reading as the Lord allows. Whether you are able to review all, some, or none of the reading and reflection, I can promise you small-group participation will always be a blessing to you. A heart bent towards the Lord's will for your life and the life of your family is all you need to bring to your small group meetings, everything else is an added personal bonus.

Throughout this study, I predominately reference the New International Version (NIV) Bible translation. However, I do occasionally reference other translations. When I use a translation other than the NIV, this will be noted after the verses referenced. The cadence and terminology vary between translations and I often find referencing varied versions brings added emphasis and understanding. Perhaps you find this too, or perhaps you have a favorite version. Whichever is your preference, feel free throughout this study to use one or many translations when looking up verses. Be assured that each worthy translation has the power to dramatically renew your life! I pray, in accordance with Scripture, that the Lord will draw you nearer throughout this study and grow your roots down deep in His marvelous love. Be blessed by The Living Bible's translation of Ephesians 3:17-19.

> And I pray that Christ will be more and more at home in your hearts, living within you as you trust in him. May your roots go down deep into the soil of God's marvelous love; and may you be able to feel and understand, as all God's children should, how long, how wide, how deep, and how high his love really is; and to experience this love for yourselves, though it is so great that you will never see the end of it or fully know or understand it. And so at last you will be filled up with God himself.

Small Group Discussion

Introductory Meeting

Believe: God will carry our burdens and calls us to carry each other's burdens.

Scripture Reading: As Christians, we come together to support each other and lift each other up in God's Word. God asks us to give our burdens to Him and to carry each other's burdens. Ask someone from the group to read these verses from Psalms, Galatians, and 1 Peter 4:10, or read them aloud in unison as a group.

> Cast your cares on the LORD, and he will sustain you;
> he will never let the righteous to be shaken.
> **Psalm 55:22**

> Carry each other's burdens, and in this way you
> will fulfill the law of Christ.
> **Galatians 6:2**

> Each of you should use whatever gift you have
> received to serve others, as faithful stewards of
> God's grace in its various forms.
> **1 Peter 4:10**

Engage: Get to know each person in your small group by taking time to introduce yourselves and talk a little bit about the roller coaster challenge you are facing with your child. This is an opportunity to begin the foundational work of building a strong group-support network.

Go around the room and encourage each person to . . .

(1) **Give his or her name.**

(2) **Give his or her child(ren)'s name(s) and the diagnosis of his or her special needs child(ren).**

(3) **Share the biggest challenge and the biggest joy they currently experience in raising their child(ren).**

(4) **Share why they are participating in this study.**

(5) **Share a specific prayer request.**

Celebrate: Praise God for bringing each person into this fellowship. He brought us together for His good purpose. He promises to be with us and He calls us to be with each other in Christ. The Lord tells us to cast our burdens on the Him and to carry each other's burdens in accordance with the gifts the Lord has given each of us. Let's celebrate the Spirit of God who guides us to the fulfillment of Scripture.

Pray: *Thank You, Lord, for being present with us. We are amazed at Your attentiveness to our burdens and grateful for the opportunity to fellowship with those who turn toward You in their challenges. Give us the grace to ease each other's troubles through prayer, companionship, and the gifts with which You have uniquely endowed each believer. We lift up each person's spoken prayer requests, and we ask the Holy Spirit to translate those yet unspoken. Strengthen our families in Christ as we meet together. Help us to grow ever more cognizant of Your renewing and powerful presence. Amen.*

(Add any specific prayer requests from group members.)

Study One – God is with Us

1.1: Where Can We Find Solutions?

In every challenge, there are numerous paths we can take in terms of solutions and strategies. This remains true for challenges involving our children, and, in particular, when we find our child has a special need significantly impacting the dreams we hold for this child. Yet while there are many paths toward helping our child progress, how we handle the challenges—in terms of behaviors and attitudes—determines if and how our child and our family thrive.

In times of trouble, as in every aspect of our lives, God gives us very specific instructions. Read what Isaiah 40 says about how God helps us in times of trouble.

> Why do you complain, Jacob?
> Why do you say, Israel,
> "My way is hidden from the Lord;
> my cause is disregarded by my God"?
> Do you not know?
> Have you not heard?
> The Lord is the everlasting God,
> the Creator of the ends of the earth.
> He will not grow tired or weary,
> and his understanding no one can fathom.
> He gives strength to the weary
> and increases the power of the weak.
> Even youths grow tired and weary,
> and young men stumble and fall;
> but those who hope in the Lord
> will renew their strength.
> They will soar on wings like eagles;
> they will run and not grow weary,
> they will walk and not be faint.
> **Isaiah 40:27-31**

They will soar on wings like eagles; they will run and not grow weary, they will walk and not be faint.
Isaiah 40:31

This passage calls us to remember that the tireless and infinite creator of the earth is concerned about the plight of the weary and weak. When we place our hope in Him, the help He gives us may come in different forms. He may grant us complete release from our troubles, allowing us to "soar on wings like eagles." Or God may give us supernatural ability to handle our trouble swiftly and energetically, allowing us to "run and not grow weary." Or God in His wisdom may not eradicate or cause us to outrun our troubles, He may instead give us the strength we need to endure them, to "walk and not be faint."

The tireless and infinite creator of the earth is concerned about the plight of the weary and weak.

> **Do one or more of these God-led trouble-conquering paths resonate with you? Take a minute to jot down one that you have recently experienced or are now experiencing.**

God is completely aware that we face enormous challenges. And He promises to be with us! In fact, the promise of His presence is the most frequent promise in the Bible. Throughout biblical history, God manifested His presence in many ways, culminating with God made flesh in Jesus, called, Immanuel, which translates to "God with us."

Whether He gives us wings to soar above our troubles, swift feet to run through them, or steady strength to endure, we can trust that He will provide what He knows is best for us in times of trouble. We simply need to receive His strength to give us the stamina to hope in, trust in, and wait on, our loving Father's way.

When my youngest daughter, Mia, was diagnosed with epilepsy and autism, my family's prayer life took on a new fervor. With so much seeming to go wrong, we really needed to feel God's presence. I wrote a lot of prose and poetry during the early years of Mia's diagnosis as a cathartic coping mechanism to help me make sense of this radically unexpected twist in my life. For my birthday one year, several friends got together a sum of money to convince me to publish these writings—which we eventually did in a book titled, *A Long Way from Shattered Glass to Mosaic.* I think of this series of writings as my version of the Psalms, for like these prayers, I express the full range of my fears, my doubts, my trust, my failures, my hopes, and my faith.

In a piece called "Categorical Panoply," I listed many of the treatment options we investigated. The word panoply means "all the arms and armor of a warrior"—which is pretty much what we, as the parents of special needs children, are seeking: all the ammunition to reach and raise our children and make sense of our lives! My husband and I waded through an extensive list of therapy options touted to "cure," or at least improve to some degree, Mia's behaviors and abilities. It was a copious, though by no means an exhaustive, list.

Categorical Panoply

A categorical panoply of vast and varied therapies
to cure or combat ASD all swim before my eyes!
And every claim I've three times read, each mixed and mingled in my
head, which one shall be our daily bread? How am I to decide?

There's Melatonin and SCD, Vitamins and DMG,
Hormones, Gluten/Casein free, and that just starts the list!
There's Feingold, Enzymes, Stimulants, Anti-psychotics, Oxidants
Prozac and other Happiants, such biochemic bliss!

There's Neurosensory Integration, Proprioceptive Stimulation
Facilitated Communication, yet, oh, indeed there's more!
There's Therapeutic Dance and Art, Hippotherapy to start,
Joint Compression to impart. What else could be in store?

Social Stories, Modeling, Chairs to spin and Chairs to swing
Psychomotor Patterning, and still so much to know!
Psycho-dynamics, ABA, Son-Rise has found another way
PECS and TEACCH and Floortime play each offer paths to go!

The options all just pile up. They fill and runneth o'er my cup;
which shall I choose to greedy sup to reach my blessed babe?
For testimonies rich abound, each method has proponents found
and I am dizzy all around. How will I find my way?

As the parent of a special needs child, I imagine your list is just as extensive. Most parents exhaust themselves exploring every avenue to help their children. Our children are that important to us!

Take a minute to create a list of all the methods you have researched as possibilities to help your child succeed.

Remember you are God's child and He is perfect in His determination to help you find your way. While we may explore hundreds of options for our children, God has unlimited ingenuity and resources at His disposal. What is God's role on your list?

If you are any small bit like me, you may have a tendency to think you can figure out ways to handle every problem. And often I will attempt to do just that before I even go to God to get His take on the situation. However, with decades of the "Mia-coaster" under my belt, God has been faithful to bring me back time and time again to His truth—God is my best resource!

Our triune God has the key to unlock every door and the wisdom to know which ones to keep shut, both here and in the heavens. Revelation 3:7 speaks of Jesus saying, "These are the words of him who is holy and true, who holds the key of David. What he opens no one can shut, and what he shuts no one can open." Let the promptings of the Spirit take an ever-larger role in directing the doors you walk toward and away from each day. Wherever you are in your ride, I can guarantee accessing God's healing and powerful presence as your most important recourse will reap amazing benefits.

1.2: The Full Armor of God

Amassing an impressive arsenal of therapies to encourage growth and life skills for our child becomes second nature to us very quickly. And just as we search out and put into practice these techniques for our children, a big part of finding our way through the special needs maze entails practicing healthy living and growth strategies for ourselves as well. I can think of no better way to stand strong in any crisis than to put on the full armor of God.

Ephesians 6:13-17 says:

> Therefore put on the full armor of God, so that when the day of evil comes, you may be able to stand your ground, and after you have done everything, to stand. Stand firm then, with the belt of truth buckled around your waist, with the breastplate of righteousness in place, and with your feet fitted with the readiness that comes from the gospel of peace. In addition to all this, take up the shield of faith, with which you can extinguish all the flaming arrows of the evil one. Take the helmet of salvation and the sword of the Spirit, which is the word of God.

Ephesians tells us that truth, righteousness, readiness from the gospel of peace, faith, and salvation are the materials that make up our God-designed armor. When we need to maintain our sanity in what often seems like completely chaotic circumstances, being clothed in God's armor is a steadying force. Understanding how to step into this armor is crucial ammunition in weathering the battles of life.

The Message translation begins this passage in Ephesians 6 with these words, "Be prepared. You're up against far more than you can handle on your own. Take all the help you can get, every weapon God has issued, so that when it's all over but the shouting you'll still be on your feet." I second this advice and use it daily myself.

Look up the verses below each concept and contemplate what God is saying about each aspect of the armor He offers us.

Truth: Jesus tells us He is the truth, and the truth will set us free.

John 14:6

Be prepared. You're up against far more than you can handle on your own. Take all the help you can get, every weapon God has issued, so that when it's all over but the shouting you'll still be on your feet.
Ephesians 6:13 (MSG)

John 8:31-32

Righteousness: Paul writes in the letter to the Romans that righteousness is acquired as a free gift through belief in Jesus Christ.

Romans 3:21-24

Romans 5:17

Readiness from the Gospel of Peace: Accepting and proclaiming the life, death, and resurrection of Jesus Christ arms us with the readiness we need.

Isaiah 52:7

Romans 10:15

Faith, Salvation, and the Word of God: Paul tells us faith comes from hearing the gospel of Christ. Anyone who hears the Word of God and confesses Christ as Savior will receive salvation.

Romans 10:8-10

Romans 10:13

Romans 10:17

Be encouraged that as believing Christians, we have all the material we need to be fully dressed in the protective covering God provides for us in battle. Let's decide together to diligently keep this holy armor wrapped about us. Let's commit to help each other fit back into place any less than secure section of our sacred armor.

1.3: Quench Your Thirst with the Word

Though it may often feel as if we have been haphazardly drafted onto this special needs ride, we do have the power to determine how we will experience it. On a roller coaster, some people are terrified, while others are exhilarated. So, the question is, "How do we get from fear to exhilaration?"

The answer has a lot to do with whether we predominately practice behaviors that embrace hopeful potential or fall into patterns that lead to the collapse of our joy, our marriages, and our families. As Christians, we can count ourselves continually blessed to have recourse to the power of faith. It can strengthen and guide us as we raise our children. I am sure I am not alone in having been given permission, in fact almost encouraged by society and errantly intentioned individuals, to find other, less steadfast, ways to handle these challenges.

Many well-meaning friends and family members have suggested coping mechanisms to me. A few of their suggestions have taken me completely off guard. I was enjoying dinner with my siblings and parents one evening when my father referred to one such outlet. He leaned in and said, "Elizabeth, I'm surprised you don't have a drinking problem." He went on to say that with all I was dealing with, not the least of which continues to be Mia's challenges, it seemed somehow supernatural that I did not NEED to drink A LOT! My father's comment was offered with a mix of humor, gravity, and paternal pride that I had not gone down that road, yet it got me thinking about the excuses we are often given, and often make, to find our peace in very questionable places.

> Make a list of the coping mechanisms that have been suggested to you, or that you have considered. Take a minute to think about the efficacy and long-term effect of each of these coping mechanisms—as positive or negative as they may be.

Whoever drinks the water I give them will never thirst. Indeed, the water I give them will become in them a spring of water welling up to eternal life.
John 4:14

Whatever our list looks like, we can thank God that one too many martinis is not the only thirst-quencher available to us. John 4:14 quotes Jesus as saying, "Whoever drinks the water I give them will never thirst. Indeed, the water I give them will become in them a spring of water welling up to eternal life."

A healthy swig of the Word is the best tonic I know. It keeps me hanging on the redemptive cross instead of hung over. Praise Jesus for offering us life! I can't claim to have never tried other methods to get through the pain such as denial, blame, anger, and self-pity. However, since God has allowed this Mia-coaster, I am confident that my surest chance of hanging on is to fully experience God securely by my side for every up, down, twist, and turn. But like all God's forgetful people, I need constant reminders that God really is with me.

Look up and write out the following verses:

Psalm 119:18

Psalm 119:105

Setting our eyes daily on His Word in Scripture provides the focus we need to see God working in our lives.

We don't need a cocktail that makes us see double. We need God to direct our gaze with His clarity. Let's partake of His Word always, and especially drink it in when life's deserts threaten to leave us high and dry. He can make visible for us the joy in store when it might otherwise be blurred amid the trials. Setting our eyes daily on His Word in Scripture provides the focus we need to see God working in our lives.

Perhaps you meditate on one Scripture each day that you have memorized or taped up where you are sure to see it. If you have never tried this, take a minute to choose one verse from our lessons thus far or find a verse that speaks to where you are right now. Tack it up on the wall, mirror, or car dashboard, somewhere you are sure to see it each day or set it up as a reminder on your mobile device. If this practice is new to you, consider sharing how this impacts your day. If you have done this often or regularly, reflect on how this enhances your daily life. In either case, consider sharing your thoughts in your next small group.

1.4: Find God in the Challenge

After Mia's diagnosis, so many things changed—from the simple to the complex. I was ill-prepared to embrace the new dynamics of grocery store outings (or any public setting for that matter), meal choices (as my daughter is highly reactive), bedtime routines, increased time with doctors and therapists (which meant significantly less time for my three older children), and a host of other lifestyle changes. As time marched on, I realized my success in navigating each instance changed dramatically, depending upon where I placed my focus. When I set my sights on worldly circumstances, I cowered, but when I set my sights on God, I was empowered! This holds true for me today.

The Lord your God goes with you; he will never leave you nor forsake you.
Deuteronomy 31:6

Be strong and courageous. Do not be afraid or terrified
because of them, for the Lord your God goes with you;
he will never leave you nor forsake you.
Deuteronomy 31:6

It is possible to let the fact that God is with us, even in the most difficult of circumstances, sink deep into the very structure and fiber of our being. It is possible to become habituated to the knowledge of His presence. God even gives us some guidance about how to do this very thing in Deuteronomy 11:18-21 when He says,

Fix these words of mine in your hearts and minds; tie them as
symbols on your hands and bind them on your foreheads. Teach them
to your children, talking about them when you sit at home and when
you walk along the road, when you lie down and when you get up.
Write them on the doorframes of your houses and on your gates.

Clearly God wants us to be constantly reminded that He is always with us—even right in the middle of our challenges. Some of us practice our own version of Deuteronomy attire and décor by wearing hats, shirts, jewelry, and bags, or decorating the walls of our homes, with Christian symbols or Scripture verses.

Do you wear or decorate your home with symbols of your faith?

Maybe you think the idea of wearing or decorating with your faith is a bit out there or maybe it's something you regularly do. In either case, how might following God's instruction to make visible His Word on our insides and our outsides be a beneficial reminder of God's presence?

Take a moment to record some especially difficult moments you have faced with your child. Note how you felt, and how you handled each situation, including your interactions with other family members or caregivers. Be completely honest, even when your reactions may have been less than saintly. Make a note if you felt God's presence in any of these challenges.

We need to know where we are starting from before we can navigate to a better place. Honest, Spirit-led reflection of our current mindset and habits goes a long way toward helping us navigate toward the light. God promises He will never leave us, and even when hardships or worries momentarily block us from sensing His presence, He is there. Scripture is full of God's assurances to His people. In Isaiah 30:19-21, He speaks through His prophet saying,

> How gracious he will be when you cry for help! As soon as he hears, he
> will answer you. Although the Lord gives you the bread of adversity and
> the water of affliction, your teachers will be hidden no more; with your own
> eyes you will see them. Whether you turn to the right or to the left, your
> ears will hear a voice behind you, saying, "This is the way; walk in it."

When we are connected to God, the strength we receive is incredible. Even when we have been disconnected for days, weeks, or years, a reconnection can give us unimaginable power. When we regularly bathe our souls in Scripture and prayer, we stretch out our hand to touch God who is always racing in earnest haste toward us.

When we regularly bathe our souls in Scripture and prayer, we stretch out our hand to touch God who is always racing in earnest haste toward us.

Immerse yourself in this scriptural prayer and ask God to help you feel His presence from the top of your head to the tips of your toes.

> LORD, you alone are my portion and my cup;
> you make my lot secure.
> The boundary lines have fallen for me in pleasant places
> surely I have a delightful inheritance.
> I will praise the LORD, who counsels me
> even at night my heart instructs me.
> I keep my eyes always on the LORD.
> With him at my right hand, I will not be shaken.
> Therefore my heart is glad and my tongue rejoices;
> my body also will rest secure,
> because you will not abandon me to the realm of the dead,
> nor will you let your faithful one see decay.
> You make known to me the path of life;
> you will fill me with joy in your presence,
> with eternal pleasures at your right hand.
> **Psalm 16:5-11**

1.5: God Is Always Working in Our Lives

Experience has taught us that this special needs roller coaster often takes much more than we think we have to give. Climbing on it was probably not an intentional life plan for most of us. But as Christians, we believe that while God does not cause the difficulties in our lives, He does allow them, and He gives us the free will to decide how we will respond to them.

Using the challenges you noted in Section 1.4's lesson, write a few words detailing how a strong belief that God is present in your challenges might change the way you handle them.

Since your child's diagnosis, how has God used the changes in your life, and your family's life, to bring positive things and/or people into your life? Are these things or people that you might not have otherwise experienced or known?

Scripture assures us repeatedly that God values us and promises to be with us always. Set aside time to ponder God's promise to be with you by reading the verses below and making a few notes under each verse about how God's promise applies to the challenges you face.

Do not be afraid; do not be discouraged,
for the LORD your God will be with you wherever you go.
Joshua 1:9

Notes:

Therefore, I tell you, do not worry about your life,
what you will eat or drink; or about your body, what you will wear.
Is not life more than food, and the body more than clothes?
Look at the birds of the air; they do not sow or reap or
store away in barns, and yet your heavenly Father feeds them.
Are you not much more valuable than they?
Matthew 6:25-26

Notes:

God is with you wherever you go. There is no place He cannot reach you. We have a God who counts us dear beyond measure. All of His children are of immensely great value to Him—that means your family and, yes, that means you too!

> *God is with you wherever you go. There is no place He cannot reach you. We have a God who counts us dear beyond measure.*

Small Group Discussion

Study One - God Is with Us

After you have individually reviewed the readings and reflection questions, meet with your small group using the suggested format below:

Believe: God is with me. His presence impacts and inspires how I react to challenges!

Scripture Reading: What does this verse mean to you?

> Fear not, for I am with you; be not dismayed, for I am your God; I will strengthen you, I will help you, I will uphold you with my righteous right hand.
>
> **Isaiah 41:10**

Engage: Review the questions below and allow each person to participate in the discussion.

1.1
- **(1) How has God enabled you to mount up with wings like eagles, run and not grow weary, or walk and not faint, when you have faced troubling times?**

- **(2) What is God's place on your list of "cure" options or management strategies for your child?**

1.2
- **(3) How does putting on the full armor of God impact how you behave as the parent of a special needs child?**

1.3
- **(4) What coping mechanisms have you tried that have failed you or fallen short?**

- **(5) How has reading, hearing, and studying Scripture lifted you up as a special needs parent?**

1.4
- **(6) What are your thoughts on wearing Christian clothing or displaying Christian symbols as a method to remind yourself whose grace you've been gifted?**

- **(7) What challenges with your child are you comfortable sharing with the group?**

- **(8) How does relying on God in your challenges impact how you face them?**

1.5

 (9) **How has God brought good to you in the midst of your challenges?**

 (10) **How does it feel to know God is with you always because He so dearly values you?**

Celebrate: Rejoice that God has solutions for us. He gives us His full armor for daily battle. His Word is our most powerful relief from stress. He is present in every challenge we face and will inspire how we address every challenge when we call on Him. He values us and is always available to us.

Pray: *We praise Your wisdom and goodness. You are the answer to every challenge. You will never leave or forsake us. Amen.*

(Add individual prayer intentions, group intentions, or revelations as appropriate from today's small group discussion.)

Trust in the LORD forever, for the LORD,
the LORD himself, is the Rock eternal.
Isaiah 26:4

STUDY TWO
GOD IS TRUSTWORTHY

Trust the Designer and Maintenance Man

In Study One you spent some time thinking about the challenges you face in raising your special needs child. I hope the verses you considered spoke to you because dwelling on our roller coaster challenges for any length of time can become overwhelming in short order. Yet as people of faith, we are called to remember that God's Word equips us for everything we face, including this unpredictable ride.

I don't know about you, but I have never boarded a roller coaster lightly. I always need to steel myself with trust in the theme park maintenance crew. I need to have reasonable confidence the roller coaster was built with careful thought and is maintained and operated for optimal safety. The prospect of boarding this supposedly entertaining ride strikes me as a monumentally treacherous endeavor.

All throughout Scripture, God's people have faced obstacles and trials. Scripture gives us intimate details about many of these challenges, and an up-close look at the fears, failings, and feats of many biblical heroes. Big or small, the difficulties in our lives often take us places we never imagined ourselves going. If God allows a hurdle in our path, we can be sure there is a glorious purpose in seeking God's assistance to go over it, under it, or through it.

23

Whether we read the Old Testament loss and triumph stories of men like Moses, David, and Job or contemplate New Testament stories of men and women who sought Jesus for healing, the Bible message is clear—all God's people endure trials of many sorts.

Through years of raising Mia, the daunting tasks I've tackled or fumbled have served to remind me of several things:

1. A trusting relationship with my faithful Father is miraculous and healing.
If I can place a hopeful trust in the theme park maintenance crew, how much more should I be able to place a steadfast trust in my faithful Father? Even though I have personally experienced the power and joy of a relationship with God, I still find myself lapsing into moments of puffed-up forgetfulness. I need His help to stay 100 percent committed to this relationship, and fortunately His very nature is faithfulness.

2. No matter how steep the climb, wisdom is offered with every step I take by His side or in His arms. I don't travel well when I journey without Him; but with Him, I am continually inspired and strengthened.

3. When my tongue and talents are bathed in His Word, God invites me to experience the joy of healing hearts. Without Him, my words and ways are just brambles and thorns; but with Him, I am blessed to be a blessing.

God has allowed us a very unique challenge in the raising of our precious children. Will we trust that He can see us through this challenge? Will we have faith in the power and skill of the Lord, the ultimate Maintenance Man, to help us do what we may believe can't be done? Will we lean with confidence on the one making the whole ride possible? And will we believe against all worldly reason that He has a spectacular ride in store for us? It is within our grasp to do so. For through the power of God's Spirit, His Word is revealed to us; and in that revelation, we receive the ability to do all these things and more.

> We do, however, speak a message of wisdom among the mature, but not the wisdom of this age or of the rulers of this age, who are coming to nothing. No, we declare God's wisdom a mystery that has been hidden and that God destined for our glory before time began. None of the rulers of this age understood it, for if they had, they would not have crucified the Lord of glory. However, as it is written: "What no eye has seen, what no ear has heard, and what no human mind has conceived," the things God has prepared for those who love him— these are the things God has revealed to us by his Spirit.
> **1 Corinthians 2:6-10**

Study Two – God Is Trustworthy

2.1: God Is in Control

When I need to anchor myself more securely to a stronghold of faith in God, I often think of this verse from Jeremiah.

> "For I know the plans I have for you," declares the Lord, "plans to prosper you and not to harm you, plans to give you hope and a future."
> **Jeremiah 29:11**

The entire Bible is God's love letter to us, promising to provide, protect, guide, lead, befriend, and save.

This verse tells me God is involved in every minute detail of my life. The more I read and pray God's Word, the stronger I become in Christ. The entire Bible is God's love letter to us, promising to provide, protect, guide, lead, befriend, and save. When we are feeling most vulnerable, God is faithful to transform brokenness, and through the healing balm of prayer much can be kept from falling into full disrepair.

> **Do you ever feel you have lost control of what is happening in your life?** ❏ yes ❏ no

Think of the last time you had to call a repair person or take your car into the shop. You knew something was wrong, but maybe you didn't know how to fix it yourself. At times like these, it's good to know someone you can trust to fix your car or your appliance. Perhaps you have someone who has proven reliable again and again. Isn't it great to know you can drop off the problem piece of machinery with confidence and let someone else expertly handle the repairs? Or perhaps you have a long-time handyman, or a tried and true company, you trust with repairs around the home. Isn't it such a relief to know that a simple phone call will bring just the help you need to the rescue?

God will meet all your needs according to the riches of his glory in Christ Jesus. 1 Peter 5:7

God tells us we can trust Him with much more than our machinery! In Philippians 4:19, Paul says, "And my God will meet all your needs according to the riches of his glory in Christ Jesus." In 1 Peter 5:7, we are told to "cast all your anxiety on him because he cares for you." God invites us to give every care to Him. After all, Jesus came so we "may have life and have it to the full" (John 10:10).

To receive this abundance, we often need to let go of our way of handling a situation. And this is rarely an easy task. Letting go of my determination to heal my daughter was the last thing I ever thought I would, or could, do. I spent years reading every book on autism I could get my hands on. I traveled the country visiting therapy centers and went down avenue after avenue in search of a cure.

Our God is not satisfied to merely address the symptoms of disrepair, He is committed to flushing out the root cause.

One day while discussing Mia with a neighbor, she called my attention to something I had not seen in myself when she put this question to me: "Elizabeth, why are you so angry lately?" Honestly, I had not even the slightest realization that I was angry though it was apparently evident to an outsider. But when she brought this to my attention, I immediately knew the answer. I had been warring in the recesses of my heart over accepting a possibility that I did not want to face—the possibility that no matter what I did, Mia may not be cured in this lifetime.

And along the way, we gain exactly what He has in mind for us— newfound freedom to enjoy an abundant life in Christ.

While letting go is as simple as releasing our perception of the way things ought to work out, it can be incredibly hard to uncurl our death grip on controlling the people and things around us. Yet, as I learned when I finally gave up trying to play Mia's savior and surrendered Christ's title back to Him, this is exactly how we move toward a stronger trust in the Lord. Our God is not satisfied to merely address the symptoms of disrepair, He is committed to flushing out the root cause and sometimes that means taking a long, circuitous route to recovery. And along the way, we gain exactly what He has in mind for us—newfound freedom to enjoy an abundant life in Christ.

List some things you would like, or know you need, to let go.

Write your prayer of trust in the space below. Ask God to help you release your grip and surrender control to Him, knowing His grip is firm, steadfast, and victorious.

We cannot trust someone we do not know, nor can we trust someone who has not proven trustworthy. But the Bible relates story after story about God's steadfast, trustworthy nature, and thereby invites us to make these stories our own personal encounters with God. In Genesis, the Bible tells us that God's original design was one of perfect harmony. I look at Mia and see absolute disharmony. This challenges me to dive deeper into Scripture, so I may become better acquainted with the One who authored what true harmony is all about. Understanding how He intended this world and its creations to interact helps me find God-ordained harmony even amid the antics of my "Mia-nator." And most important, Scripture assures me my God, who does what He says He is going to do, has plans to restore my life to one of perfect harmony.

> *Scripture assures me my God, who does what He says He is going to do, has plans to restore my life to one of perfect harmony.*

Do you have a favorite story in the Bible that demonstrates God does what He says He will do? If so, list a few details from this story.

Now, take a minute to read Exodus 6:6 and consider whether God proved trustworthy to do as He promised in this verse. Relate a few details that demonstrate God's trustworthy nature.

God's miraculous interventions in the lives of our scriptural ancestors are building blocks of faith. They are meant to be passed on to every succeeding generation. He still moves and shows up in our lives today.

If you have a personal story about how He has proven trustworthy to you, write some notes detailing this below.

Your God-stories serve the dual purpose of both personal and community faith builders. God is gracious to show up and show off specifically to give our faith a caffeine jolt of grand proportion. Let's open our eyes to both the subtle and the outrageous ways God orchestrates the various elements of each day, for in so doing, we experience His brilliant and loving presence.

2.2: Expect Challenges

In the world you will have trouble. But take heart! I have overcome the world.
John 16:33

Consider that God has been trustworthy in warning you that challenges were coming into your life. John 16:33 says, "I have told you these things, so that in me you may have peace. In the world you will have trouble. But take heart! I have overcome the world." And, 1 Peter 4:12 tells us, "Dear friends, do not be surprised at the fiery ordeal that has comes on you to test you, as though something strange were happening to you."

Perhaps you have experienced a particular difficulty this week or in the not too distant past. If so, how did this impact your mood, your outlook, your way of handling everything else?

If someone asked you to describe the more difficult aspects of your week with two or three adjectives, what would those be?

God's Word acknowledges we will face trials, but He also assures us we will not suffer indefinitely. First Peter 5:10 says, "And the God of all grace, who called you to his eternal glory in Christ, after you have suffered a little while, will himself restore you and make you strong, firm and steadfast." When I have lifted up earnest prayers in some very dark hours, 1 Peter 5:10 has been an enormously comforting Scripture. These dark hours have been many in our journey with Mia, and time and time again God has been true to His Word. He has helped me shift my definition of "a little while" to one representing a time frame in line with His promises. Mia has had autism for many years now, but God constantly offers respite from its burdens in surprising ways. And I know the ultimate respite will be to witness a wholly healed Mia in heaven. Still, the Lord has also provided some tangible restoration in the here and now concerning the many physical complications of her disability.

During one particularly unfathomable period of two and one-half years, Mia suffered screaming seizures 3 to 10 times each and every night. The downward spiral began with drop-seizures at school which led to the loss of speech, weight, body function control, energy, and emotional display. It was a horrific time for our entire family as we habituated to waking many times each night to Mia's screams—no easy jolt from sleep, I assure you. In fact, Mia slept with one of us each night so that we could help her through these seizures. Then one day, as suddenly as they began, the seizures just stopped.

You see, God was quite literal in His message to us on this one, for after this first evening in two and a half years in which Mia slept undisturbed by seizures, God restored us all through a restful night's sleep and joy in the morning over Mia's miraculous healing. We had indeed suffered a little while, and then the God of all grace, faithful to His Word, restored and strengthened us.

And along with strength and restoration, God promises to provide the way of escape and deliverance. First Corinthians 10:13 says, "No temptation has overtaken you except what is common to mankind. And God is faithful; he will not let you be tempted beyond what you can bear. But when you are tempted, he will also provide a way out so that you can endure it." The ESV words it slightly differently saying God, "will also provide the way of escape."

When I first read this verse, I was struck with how very different its meaning was from what I had heard from the lips of earnest comforters who referred to it. The Scripture does not say we will never be given more than we can handle. Rather, it says when we are overcome by more than we can handle and tempted to despair, God will provide a way out, a way of escape, allowing us to endure it. I know the only way we made it through that two and a half-year period of Mia's seizures was because God granted us many moments of joy and profound connection in which we found escape from the difficulty.

> **Share a few details below about an especially intense period of suffering you have endured or are enduring.**

> **When challenges overwhelm us, the Christian response is prayer. Are you waiting to hear from God about something for which you have been praying?**

Has God answered a particular prayer? If so, were your prayers answered as you expected or asked? Or were your prayers answered in a way different from what you expected or asked?

When we call on God, He always answers. I have experienced Him saying, "Yes, right now," "Yes, but not now," "Yes, but in another way," and "No, I have something better." I may not always adequately appreciate God's "wait a bit" or "no" answers; in fact, I may even classify them as the beginning of very bad days long before I understand the full glory of His answer. As Christians, we believe God created the heavens and the earth and every living creature in them, surely we can trust Him to recreate our lives no matter how shattered we may feel they have become. God can teach us in the plunges, inspire us on the peaks, and keep us firmly on the track, even when we think we might fly right off!

When we call on God, He always answers. I have experienced Him saying, "Yes, right now," "Yes, but not now," "Yes, but in another way," and "No, I have something better."

> As for God, his way is perfect: The LORD's word is flawless;
> he shields all who take refuge in him.
> **Psalm 18:30**

He will lead us safely, no matter what this broken world hurls at us, no matter how rickety, frightening, and uncertain our ride appears. But, we must believe His Word, because our power comes from what we believe. And what we believe determines whether the power we wield heals or hurts. When we believe in lies, our power can be zapped or become deadly. When we believe His Word, we are empowered to do mountains of good.

We must believe His Word, because our power comes from what we believe. And what we believe determines whether the power we wield heals or hurts.

In facing the duties of parenting your child, think about where you are placing your trust. On a scale of 1-10, how much are you leaning on a particular course of treatment and education, a doctor, support team, more money to secure treatment for your child, your spouse to help carry the load, or your own determination to cure your child?

On that same scale, how much are you leaning on God and trusting in His good plan for you, your child, and your family?

The impulsive, unconventional nature of Mia's autism was the big push that helped me realize I was fooling myself to have ever thought I was in control of my life. I never was and never would be—I just didn't notice this as much before Mia. I also realized I was fooling myself to attempt to lean on anything with more weight than I leaned on God. Post-Mia, I have found that trusting in God's ability to turn ashes into beauty, to bring good from evil, has become my sustaining power. Prayer is a constant, and I have discovered God to be gracious in providing surprising and touching responses to prayer.

Have you ever experienced a time when life felt completely out of balance, yet God was giving you great peace?

Write a simple prayer from the heart asking God to open your eyes to what He has done, and is doing, to affect your circumstances and your heart amidst the struggle.

2.3: More Than a Gold Star

When children are small, the success of a school day is often measured in terms of what color star they earned. As they age, the measurement changes to what grade they receive on a test or homework. The school assessments Mia's teachers have always sent home measure her days in terms of how appropriately she regulated her volume, how well she controlled her impulsivity, and how many elopements she managed from the classroom.

In case you are wondering, as I did when Mia's teachers first used the phrase, what an "elopement" means for a special needs child, this is one dictionary definition I came across: "An elopement is an act or instance of leaving a safe area or safe premises, done by a person with a mental disorder or cognitive impairment: Parents of autistic children need strategies to cope with elopement." I second that: we do indeed need strategies, but we also need better measurements.

As special needs parents, we often measure our lives in terms of how "normal" or "not so normal" our family life was today or how close or far our children are to the milestones of their peers. All measuring sticks can be emotionally draining. But when we regularly fall short, they are downright demoralizing.

We all have yes and no days, good and bad days. And in those no or bad days, most of us need far more patience than we are often able to muster. Some of us measure our days in funny ways. We often joke about good or bad hair days, skinny jean or comfy sweats days, happy or miserable children days, tough or easy commute days, good or bad sports performance days, optimal or minimal work-accomplished days, well-planned or way too many unexpected-events days, parent-of-the-year or parental failure days, and jackpot or hardly made-a-dime days. However, because whatever measurements we use moment to moment can leave us feeling we are living a well-done, all-around life or a missing-the-mark life, it is important to be aware of and evaluate the impact and usefulness of these measures.

> **Take a moment to list some of the standards you are using to measure the kind of days you've had this week.**

Our feelings about our days, weeks, and years vary and vacillate constantly. The intensity and duration of the vacillations can be directly impacted by the measures we use to judge our lives. Our changing circumstances and emotions are not in and of themselves problematic, for even the Bible in Ecclesiastes 3 tells us there is a time and season for everything.

There is a time for everything,
and a season for every activity under the heavens:
a time to be born and a time to die,
a time to plant and a time to uproot,
a time to kill and a time to heal,
a time to tear down and a time to build,
a time to weep and a time to laugh,
a time to mourn and a time to dance,
a time to scatter stones and a time to gather them,
a time to embrace and a time to refrain from embracing,
a time to search and a time to give up,
a time to keep and a time to throw away,
a time to tear and a time to mend,
a time to be silent and a time to speak,
a time to love and a time to hate,
a time for war and a time for peace.

Ecclesiastes 3:1-8

Therefore do not worry about tomorrow, for tomorrow will worry about itself. Each day has enough trouble of its own. Matthew 6:34

This Scripture certainly rings true in my life, and I imagine it does in yours as well. However, without a proper measuring stick, these normal ups and downs of life can wreak mental, physical, and social havoc. On the special needs roller coaster ride, the typical lows may feel more precipitous, while the highs may feel more elevated. So, what does that mean in terms of experiencing the rest of your life with a special needs child? Well, I have learned that I cannot think in terms of what Mia will be like 'for the rest of her life,' nor can I think in terms of what I will be required to manage in terms of Mia 'for the rest of my life.' These are contemplations I simply have no business entertaining, because, while I really have no idea what lies ahead, I do know where this kind of thinking will lead me. And more important, Scripture is quite specific concerning what I should be dwelling on each day. Jesus assures us that He is looking out for us and then says in Matthew 6:34, "Therefore do not worry about tomorrow, for tomorrow will worry about itself. Each day has enough trouble of its own."

So rather than worldly comparisons, I have come to see that the truest, most useful, and up-building measure of my day relies on how much I actively pay attention to what God is saying and doing throughout that day. When we focus on God's scriptural promise to be with us every step of the way, the certainty of His hand on every aspect of our lives is superior to any gold star we might receive or award ourselves for accomplishing any particular task. God's touch is pure. It can lead to tears, tingles, laughs, sighs, and speechless awe. It is the only measure that lifts even when we fall short.

> **Read the story of Elisha and his servant in 2 Kings 6:8-22. Then note below if there were any verses or details in this story that stood out for you. If so, why did they capture your attention?**

God's touch is pure. It can lead to tears, tingles, laughs, sighs, and speechless awe. It is the only measure that lifts even when we fall short.

My favorite verses in this story are: "Don't be afraid," the prophet answered. "Those who are with us are more than those who are with them." And Elisha prayed, "Open his eyes, Lord, so that he may see." Then the Lord opened the servant's eyes, and he looked and saw the hills full of horses and chariots of fire all around Elisha (2 Kings 6:16-17).

These verses remind me that God-work is going on around me all the time. When I become consumed with my own to-do list at the expense of His, I know it is time to slow down and ask God to open these tired, near-sighted eyes. The translation in the New King James Version (NKJV) is powerful as it quotes Paul giving God glory.

> Now to him who is able to do exceedingly abundantly above all that
> we ask or think, according to the power that works in us, to him be glory in
> the church by Christ Jesus to all generations, forever and ever. Amen.
> **Ephesians 3:20-21 NKJV**

I love the thought that the Lord is able and willing to do 'exceedingly abundantly above' what we have the capacity to ask or imagine in our lives.

Ask God to help you visualize a time when He worked, or is working now, in a marvelous way to impact your life. Then, detail the circumstances below.

The Lord is able and willing to do 'exceedingly abundantly above' what we have the capacity to ask or imagine in our lives.

Trust God with all your ups and downs. Invite Him to open your eyes and wow you! Let your attentiveness to His work be your truest measure of success.

2.4: God Knows Our Thoughts

God is working even when we are not aware that He is, even when we are not actively inviting Him to do so.

Thankfully, God is working even when we are not aware that He is, even when we are not actively inviting Him to do so. He knows the words that come out of our mouths daily. He knows them before we speak them. As Psalm 139 demonstrates, He knows them even when we never consciously speak them.

> You have searched me, LORD, and you know me.
> You know when I sit and when I rise; you perceive my thoughts from afar.
> You discern my going out and my lying down; you are familiar with all my ways.
> Before a word is on my tongue you, LORD, know it completely.
> **Psalm 139:1-4**

God knows exactly how and when He ought to respond proactively and reactively for our greatest good. His methods of reaching out to us prove He hears our thoughts and knows our words. Let me share a memorable time when God anticipated my thoughts.

As I imagine many of you have experienced, caring for a special needs child is particularly draining in many areas, including your finances. In my family of six, Mia's needs took quite a toll on our bank accounts and affected our working lives and the educational and recreational lives of our older children. It rocked all of our worlds. Over the course of one particular week, I had amassed quite a collection of bills to be paid and was greatly concerned over how we would manage. Even with countless biblical assurances of God's provision, I admit to being part of the stiff-necked people crowd that God fusses at in the Old Testament. Too often I let worries mount and get the best of me.

On the last day of the week, as I walked from the house to the mailbox, I prayed a "Gideon prayer." You know the story about the fleece. Gideon wanted a sign to be sure he was on the right track and had really heard God correctly. Let's push pause on my story for just a minute; I promise I won't leave you hanging for long. But now is the perfect time to take a minute to read Gideon's story.

Read Judges 6:11-40 now, paying careful attention to Gideon's requests in verses 36-40 at the end of this text. After reading the passage, consider if you have ever prayed a Gideon-type prayer and jot your thoughts below.

Read just the portion from Judges 6:36-40 one more time: Gideon said to God,

"If you will save Israel by my hand as you have promised — look, I will place a wool fleece on the threshing floor. If there is dew only on the fleece and all the ground is dry, then I will know that you will save Israel by my hand, as you said." And that is what happened. Gideon rose early the next day; he squeezed the fleece and wrung out the dew—a bowlful of water. Then Gideon said to God, "Do not be angry with me. Let me make just one more request. Allow me one more test with the fleece, but this time make the fleece dry and let the ground be covered with dew." That night God did so. Only the fleece was dry; all the ground was covered with dew.

Gideon was both bold and needy in his request to a God who had already provided ample proof that He was with Gideon in this matter. And God obliged His child for He loved him dearly and had a great work in store for Gideon. You and I are no different. We are His dearly loved children. When we find ourselves in need of His reassurance, we are told we can go boldly to the throne through Christ.

> *We are His dearly loved children. When we find ourselves in need of His reassurance, we are told we can go boldly to the throne through Christ.*

Perhaps you have, at one time or another, found yourself praying a Gideon prayer. In light of the financial uncertainty I described, this was the essence of the Gideon prayer that poured from my lips, "God, I know you are there. I know you have promised to provide. But could I trouble you for a small sign, just a dollar in the mailbox today, instead of all those bills. Even with all the assurance you have given me, Father, I implore you for this small sign that all will be well." It is not a long walk to the mailbox at the end of our drive, but I walked slowly and prayed with heartfelt passion and petition that God, beyond all the scriptural and real-life assurance He had already graciously extended me, would grant me this additional small sign.

Upon opening the mailbox, I found a hand-addressed envelope with no return address. When I opened the envelope, a $6,000 check met my eyes. Not a dollar, not $10, but $6,000! I was awed to tears as I read the card relating how my husband and I had lent my sister-in-law a sum of money seven years ago, and when she had tried to repay us, we had told her to keep the money. She explained that she had kept it and put it in a savings account. It had accrued interest and something in her told her we might just need this money now. I was truly stunned. God knew I would make this very plea, on this very day. He knew the words I would speak and had been at work in another's heart to provide me a "yes and something so much more than you asked for" answer to prayer. Isn't He just amazing?

> **Relate a time or times God anticipated your words or thoughts. Use the space below, or a separate piece of paper, to make notes about as many of these moments as you can recall. If you have trouble recalling a particular time, pray a Gideon prayer and ask Him to show you that He hears you even before you speak.**

When God works in our lives, each instance can become one of our personal stones of remembrance. Stones are weighty, sturdy, and durable. They give us something solid to focus on when our doubts threaten to make us forget. When we find a way to visibly commemorate God's work in our lives, stone upon stone, we erect a great memorial anchoring our thoughts and our hearts to His.

2.5: He Will Teach Us His Word

God is a faithful guide. He has given us His Spirit. His Spirit reveals God's Word guiding us to truth. Scripture will always be in harmony with whatever has been truly revealed to us by the Spirit.

But when he, the Spirit of truth, comes, he will guide
you into all the truth. He will not speak on his own; he will speak
only what he hears, and he will tell you what is yet to come.

John 16:13

When Mia was young, she had the perseverating habit of lobbing small objects repetitively just for the satisfaction of seeing them fly. One day I was in her room, putting her freshly laundered clothes away, while she was lining up small plastic animal figures. She started firing the figures in my direction. No matter the patience with which I asked her to redirect her aim, she continued to pitch with perfection at my head and shoulders over and over again. In complete exasperation, I picked up one of the fallen toys with every intention of hurling it back her way to give her a good dose of her own medicine. Not one of my finer moments.

Fortunately, though, I didn't even think to ask, the toy never left my hand, because God had a message for me. His gentle but powerful words rang loud and clear in my ears: *The angels of my little ones stare straight at the face of God.* You will not be surprised to learn that I laid my body right down on Mia's bedroom floor and wept with remorse, thanksgiving, and petition. I prayed that God would grant me too the vision of His glorious face whenever I looked upon my own daughter. I needed to see what I perceived as Mia's mindless madness as something entirely different. I needed to see it as a way to see God so that He could transform a pattern of responding to Mia's frustrating behaviors with frustrating behaviors of my own to a pattern of responding to them with prayer and an opportunity to seek the face of God.

Shortly thereafter, I found the verse God spoke to me in Matthew 18:10. Look it up and write it out now for yourself.

Matthew 18:10:

How differently we might perceive each relationship encounter if we could envision the face of God when we look at every person in our lives. In fact, imagine how different our approach to all of life might be if every line of Scripture was etched on our hearts. The following verse is found in three places in the Bible, and the concept is paraphrased in many other verses; "I will put my law in their minds and write it on their hearts" (Jeremiah 31:33, Hebrews 8:10 and 10:16).

> **Look up Isaiah 30:21 and John 6:63. In the space below, personalize them as a message from God to you.**

God's Word is life and He will make sure we hear it!

> **Relate a time when a verse of Scripture was presented to you at just the right moment—in a sermon, by another person, in a Bible study, in a whisper from the Spirit. What was its effect?**

God can be trusted to act in our lives for our good.

God can be trusted to act in our lives for our good. He manifests His presence when people are aware and even when we are unaware. But it is so much more fun to be expecting and watching for Him to work in our lives. I imagine we are all praying for healing in our children with every ounce of our being. Along with prayers for complete healing, I had also been praying that the Lord would grant me some glimpse of a capacity for compassion in my impulsively aggressive daughter. After many years of this focused prayer, the Lord answered my plea.

It was a lovely summer afternoon and my family was spending it at our neighborhood pool. I was with Mia near the baby pool. My husband and three older daughters were playing in the larger pool. There were a few mothers with their much younger children around the baby pool as well. And then, just like that, on an ordinary day, my years of petition were answered and a piece of my heart was mended. I started whooping with excitement and called my husband and children over to witness the scene. We were all making quite a fuss and a mother sitting nearby looked completely perplexed at our elation. After all, my daughter had only comforted a crying toddler by offering him the toy she was playing with—a simple act for many children. Yet, what could this mother know of my child's years of complete indifference to the pain of others, of her penchant for sudden violence. My smile broadened in response to her confusion, for in that moment, my family was proud beyond any observer's understanding to count our daughter, at last, among the compassionate.

Perhaps you too have experienced that the joy we feel over the development of a "neurotypical" child is made a hundredfold more jubilant when our special needs child achieves a developmental milestone. Though I never saw any indication of it until this blessed day, God was brewing up a special brand of compassion for my Mia, and He chose that moment to reveal it to us. My family was completely swept up in the joy of that God-designed moment.

I am still asking God to heal Mia, I will never stop petitioning Him. He has healed her in many incremental ways, and though he has not fully healed her, He continues to heal me and many others through Mia. In His answers to petitions I habitually offer up for Mia, He has shown me His glory through His "no, not yet," and "no, not that, but this" just as surely as He has shown it in His "yes" and "yes, but more." And Scripture assures me that "our present sufferings are not worth comparing with the glory that will be revealed in us" (Romans 8:18).

He has shown me His glory through His "no, not yet," and "no, not that, but this" just as surely as He has shown it in His "yes" and "yes, but more."

I know God will heal our children, whether it is in this life or the next, because Scripture gives us this promise from the hand of John the Revelator:

> And I heard a loud voice from the throne saying, "Look! God's
> dwelling place is now among the people, and he will dwell with them.
> They will be his people, and God himself will be with them and be their God.
> 'He will wipe every tear from their eyes. There will be no more death' or mourning
> or crying or pain, for the old order of things has passed away." He who was
> seated on the throne said, "I am making everything new!" Then he said,
> "Write this down, for these words are trustworthy and true."
> **Revelation 21:3-5**

Think about all the ways God has shown He is with you and can be trusted. If you find this hard to do, simply spend this week talking to Him, praying and being open to what He wants to show you. You will not be disappointed. God is faithful, and there is no end to the marvels He wants to share with you!

Small Group Discussion

Study Two - God Is Trustworthy

After you have individually reviewed the readings and reflection questions, meet with your small group using the suggested format below:

Believe: We can trust God to show up in our challenges.

Scripture Reading: What does this verse mean to you?

> The righteous cry out, and the LORD hears them; he delivers them from all their troubles.
> The LORD is close to the brokenhearted and saves those who are crushed in spirit.
> **Psalm 34:17-18**

Engage: Review the questions below and allow each person to participate in the discussion.

2.1

(1) Share situations in which you felt you did not, or do not, have any control of what is happening in your life.

(2) What things do you, or did you, need to let go and entrust to the Lord?

(3) How has God proven trustworthy in your life? What did He do in Exodus 6:6?

2.2

(4) What prayers are you waiting to hear from God on and how do you feel about waiting?

(5) How has God answered specific prayers in ways you have or have not expected?

(6) How have you experienced God's peace even in the middle of significant trials?

2.3

(7) What measure do you use to determine the success of your day/life?

(8) How have God's miraculous interventions shaped how you view your life?

2.4

(9) Share a 'Gideon prayer' you have prayed or would like to pray.

(10) How has God made you confident that He knows your heart and knows what is on your tongue before you speak it?

2.5

(11) Share moments you were presented with a scriptural reminder at the exact moment you needed to hear it.

Celebrate: Praise God for He assures us that even though challenges will come, He will provide the way of escape. He knows our thoughts and teaches us His Word. He opens our eyes to moments of joy and is faithful to guide us toward the good.

Pray: *Lord, grant us the grace to trust You completely. Open our eyes to all You are doing in our lives. Write Your Word on our hearts and in our minds. Help us be doers of Your Word. Amen.*

(Address prayer concerns or important points of prayer from today's small group discussion.)

For the Spirit God gave us does
not make us timid, but gives us
power, love and self-discipline.
2 Timothy 1:7

GOD GIVES US A SPIRIT OF COURAGE

Activate Your Spirit of Courage

What happens when we are afraid? Speaking from personal experience, fear has caused me to feel cautious, suspicious, powerless, angry, or to blame others and lose control. Perhaps you have a similar list of the emotional places fear has taken you. Yet, Scripture tells us we need not fear; in fact, 2 Timothy 1:7 says God gave us a Spirit that is the exact opposite of fear. It is one of power, love, and self-control. So, when fear begins to seep into our thoughts, we have the ability to actualize our God-given Spirit and overcome fear with these divine gifts.

Yet, so often we give in to fear, especially in difficult situations concerning our children. What can we do that will allow us to channel this fear into a reminder to call on the Spirit of God within? Like so many of us, I have found the only way I can replace one habitual pattern of reaction with another is by actively and thoughtfully asking God to change the way I think about a situation. When I study how God thinks about a situation, apply it, and pray His words, then I am allowing Him to take all my thoughts captive. And I am confident there is no better manager of my thoughts than my wise and all-loving Father. As people of faith, God assures He has given us the power to overcome our fears.

Let's think about where we get faith to begin with by looking at the Scripture references below:

• Ephesians 2:8 tells us: "For it is by grace you have been saved, through faith—and this is not from yourselves, it is the gift of God." **So, faith is a gift from God.**

• Romans 12:3 says, "Think of yourself with sober judgment, in accordance with the faith God has distributed to each of you." **So, we know God has offered each of us the gift of faith.**

• Romans 10:17 says, "Faith comes from hearing the message, and the message is heard through the word about Christ." **So, we know that God offers us the gift of faith through the Word of Christ.**

• Hebrews 12:2 calls Jesus, "The pioneer and perfecter of faith," and 2 Peter 3:18 encourages us to "grow in the grace and knowledge of our Lord and Savior Jesus Christ." **So, when we hear and study the Word, we grow our faith, which is perfected by Christ.**

Receiving God's Word is clearly powerful. Christ is the embodiment of the Word of God. We know from our previous study that God promises to be with us, and He is trustworthy. He wants His Word to be alive in us. In Hebrews 10:16, we read about God saying, "I will put my laws in their hearts, and . . . write them on their minds." He desires for us to know His Word in a very intimate way, and thereby know Him.

When studying, reading, or reciting Scripture is a habitual part of our lives, it infuses every tendency, habit, and experience with divine revelation. The Holy Spirit also speaks the Word into our lives. In John 14:26 Jesus said, "the Holy Spirit, whom the Father will send in my name, will teach you all things and will remind you of everything I have said to you."

Let's join our voices to Paul's and pray for each other from Ephesians 1:17-19:

I keep asking that the God of our Lord Jesus Christ, the glorious Father,
may give you the Spirit of wisdom and revelation, so that you may know him better.
I pray that the eyes of your heart may be enlightened in order that you may know the hope
to which he has called you, the riches of his glorious inheritance in his holy people,
and his incomparably great power for us who believe.

STUDY THREE – GOD GIVES US A SPIRIT OF COURAGE

3.1: Be Not Afraid

God wants us to move from simply reading about the God of the Bible to personally experiencing the God of the Bible. We can, in fact, experience God moving, acting, and speaking in our lives. God reaches out to us when we need Him and even when we don't acknowledge we need Him. He wants us to access our courage through our relationship with Him.

Are there any areas of your life where fear is preventing you from experiencing God moving, acting, and speaking in your life?

If you, like me, were able to list an area or two; take heart, because we know we are not alone. Even God's most accomplished biblical heroes faced moments of fear. In fact, reminding His people not to be afraid is a frequent scriptural message.

Look up these verses and note under which specific circumstances God is encouraging His people.

Be strong and courageous. Do not be afraid or terrified
because of them, for the LORD your God goes with you;
he will never leave you nor forsake you.
Deuteronomy 31:6

Circumstance:

Have I not commanded you? Be strong and courageous.
Do not be afraid; do not be discouraged, for the LORD your
God will be with you wherever you go.
Joshua 1:9

Circumstance:

David also said to Solomon his son, "Be strong and courageous,
and do the work. Do not be afraid or discouraged, for the LORD God,
my God, is with you. He will not fail you or forsake you until all the work
for the service of the temple of the LORD is finished.
1 Chronicles 28:20

Circumstance:

Overhearing what they said, Jesus told him,
"Don't be afraid; just believe."
Mark 5:36

Circumstance:

When a revelation you receive is consistent with God's Word, you can be confident that God is reaching out in intimate ways to strengthen your faith.

God's scriptural command "to be strong and fear not" is meant as much for us today as it was for our ancestors. God never stops revealing Himself to us. When a revelation you receive is consistent with God's Word, you can be confident that God is reaching out in intimate ways to strengthen your faith. Acts 17:11 tells us the importance of checking revelation against Scripture as it claimed that the Berean Jews "were of more noble character than those in Thessalonica, for they received the message with great eagerness and examined the Scriptures every day to see if what Paul said was true."

Where do you turn for assurance when you are afraid? What do you do to alleviate your fears? Consider whether your answers to the questions above are consistent with what God's Word tells us about conquering fear.

God tells us the surest way to overcome fear is to be confident that He is with us! Thus far in our study, we have spent considerable time studying His assurances that He is both with us and trustworthy. To be truly confident of His presence and promises, we need to know Him. And to know Him, we need to know His Word.

> Spend a few minutes in prayer asking God to solidify your confidence in Him. Ask Him to write His Word on your heart so you'll have all you need to pole vault over your fears.

3.2: Faith

Faith is the key to unlocking ever deeper doors of a trusting and courage-building relationship with God. We've talked about how we receive faith and how we grow and perfect faith, but what is faith?

> Write out your personal definition of faith, perhaps including your favorite scriptural reference.

Hebrews 11:1 tells us, "Now faith is confidence in what we hope for and assurance about what we do not see." The NKJV translates Hebrews 11:1 slightly differently, "Faith is the substance of things hoped for, the evidence of things not seen."

Now faith is confidence in what we hope for and assurance about what we do not see.
Hebrews 11:1

Let me share a story about a time I intimately experienced this scriptural definition of faith. To help Mia operate in the world, we were constantly looking for ways to turn the odd things she did into behaviors that looked more typical. So, one day as she was marching in repetitive circles, head down, banging two, similarly weighted and shaped, objects together and humming to herself, I joined her by mimicking exactly what she was doing and saying, "Wow, I love playing marching band with you." Now Mia was most definitely not playing marching band, but for the first time in her life she looked over at me with interest as if to say, "Hey, you like to do what I like to do." The reward of that first eye-to-eye contact was motivation enough to keep us all pretending she was playing

God tells us we need only a small mustard-seed-sized faith to accomplish amazing things.

marching band until, eventually, we were able to offer her cymbals and a drum to bang—and then—she actually was playing marching band! The point is we all pretended to see what we did not see until we actually saw it!

That is how it is with faith. You start with one small step and grow your faith through scriptural revelation. God tells us we need only a small mustard-seed-sized faith to accomplish amazing things.

> The apostles said to the Lord, "Increase our faith!"
> He replied, "If you have faith as small as a mustard seed,
> you can say to this mulberry tree, 'Be uprooted and planted
> in the sea,' and it would obey you."
> **Luke 17:5-6**

How would you compare the size of your faith to a mustard seed?

A mustard seed is a truly small seed, and yet what God is telling us is that even a smidgen of faith is enough to uproot any stubborn obstacle.

That may not be an easy question to answer; in fact, in God's seed-planting world, if we have any faith at all, the size of our faith is almost completely irrelevant. A mustard seed is a truly small seed, and yet what God is telling us is that even a smidgen of faith is enough to uproot any stubborn obstacle. If you are participating in this study, I can guarantee you have all the faith you need to overcome fear.

When we believe God's Word and promises—believe even what we cannot see—His Word comes alive in us and our spiritual eyes are opened. With open eyes, we really can see God at work in our lives. And when we see how He is working, we are strengthened, empowered, and emboldened. God strengthened me through Mia's display of compassion, His answer to my "Gideon prayer," and His message to see His face when I look upon my daughter. He continues to work in my life through Bible studies, Sunday sermons and daily displays of His presence. When I witness God at work something vital to my ability to live this epileptically autistic life is ignited and enlarged—that something is my faith. And this faith is not weightless, it has substance and evidence. Its substance is **_"of things hoped for"_** and its evidence is **_"of things not seen."_**

Pay careful attention to this grouping of scriptural words. Note that the things hoped for have **substance** when we hope for them in Christ! And not only is faith defined as something with substance, but also as something with **evidence**. This tells us our hope is not built on imaginary fairy tales but on something, and even someone, substantial and provable. What could be more substantial or provide more evidence than hearing from God and witnessing the fulfillment of His promises?

While it may take some degree of courage to board an amusement park roller coaster, it is always our choice to board or not to board. This is not so with the special needs roller coaster—this is a ride we have literally been shoved on. Yet even here, we still have choices. We can choose to see what can't be seen with the eyes of the world. Like the story about Elisha and his servant you read in Study Two, our eyes can be opened to the unbelievably miraculous power we are harnessed to in Christ. And in so seeing, we can choose to ride this roller coaster with the courage of faith.

> **Consider whether you have accessed your God-given Spirit of courage in the face of a difficult situation in your life, and then list some details of this circumstance below. If you need God's help to utilize the Spirit He has given you, spend some time in prayer asking for this.**

3.3: Hope Is Essential to Faith

I have heard it said we can go 40 days without food, three days without water, and eight minutes without air, but we cannot even live one minute without hope in something or someone. This makes sense to me given some of the very difficult situations I have endured—in each instance, even if I had to give up "this earthly lifetime" hope in one area of my life, I held onto my hope in Jesus because I knew to lose that hope was to lose everything. Studies of people who have survived very difficult, and even horrific situations, such as concentration camps, war, or natural disaster show that these people endured because they held on to hope.

Answered prayers are the incredible evidence pointing to God's care in our lives.

Many of us have had times in our lives where we have gone without things, perhaps even essential things, like food, sleep, health, financial provision, or companionship. And if you are engaged in this study, you have most likely experienced the struggles of raising a special needs child. What keeps, or kept, you going through these tough times? What are you, or were you, hoping for?

A special needs diagnosis for your child is a one-way ticket to difficult times, yet with God we can turn it into the most rewarding ride of our lives. The hope that God will turn things around can keep us moving onward against all odds. In fact, despite the monumental challenges of raising special needs children, we are all very much proof of the power of hope. I imagine you, like me, continue to hope there are better days ahead. In a sense, the substance of things hoped for in our lives is staring back at us every day when we look in the mirror—our very existence and daily breath is proof of our hope.

There are many things I have hoped for which have taken on substance in my life. Things like landing a job, growing closer with my spouse, the miracle of my children, regained health, and financial provision. Answered prayers are the incredible evidence pointing to God's care in our lives. Let's commit to being attentive to how the things we hope for take on very real substance.

List things in your life that have taken on substance and demonstrate the things you have hoped for.

Consider the reasonableness of placing limits on what is okay for any person to hope for in life. Is it possible that some of us unwittingly let ourselves believe in limits of our own making that prevent us from realizing all God has for us? Write your thoughts below.

Let's ask God to help us wear our "hope" in Christ like a cloak of optimism, believing there will be something of substance to gain in every situation. Our lives can be thrilling even in the chaos of unexpected twists and turns. God can rock our world in wonderful ways. With God's help, we can make a conscious decision that the gains we will make are worth the heartache, the loss, the risk. When we embrace hope as the Spirit who says there will be light in this darkness, we are embracing the light of Christ, for He alone is our hope and salvation.

When we embrace hope as the Spirit who says there will be light in this darkness, we are embracing the light of Christ, for He alone is our hope and salvation.

May the God of hope fill you with all joy and
peace as you trust in him, so that you may overflow with
hope by the power of the Holy Spirit.
Romans 15:13

3.4: The One Jesus Loves

When we hope in Christ, we hope in someone very substantial. God became man and walked with us in real flesh and blood. Jesus is 100 percent God and 100 percent man. His life, death, and resurrection are the proof of our great hope in an eternal blissful life. Christ is the most important substance and evidence of our faith. Imagine what it must have been like to walk with Him in the flesh. What assurance it must have been to touch Him and be touched by Him. And what bliss to adore Him in the flesh and be adored by Him.

John captures what I imagine it was like in his gospel. The Gospel of John is the only Gospel to use the phrase, "The disciple whom Jesus loved." Have you ever wondered why the apostle John refers to himself so often as the one Jesus loved? Scripture makes it clear he was not inferring that Christ loved the other disciples less than He loved John. In fact, it is more probable that John was standing firm on words of Scripture telling us we are each created to be uniquely and unconditionally loved by God.

We are each created to be uniquely and unconditionally loved by God.

Considering that Christ is the most substantial and trustworthy being alive, how fortunate for us that we are all God's unique favorites. He loves us in a way that is specific to each of us as He accompanies us on this ride of terror and wonder. He will never leave us or forsake us. This hope is true. And this hope gives us courage. His Word assures us of this.

Has there ever been a time in your life when you have wondered if God really loves you?

On one Sunday morning, I had been battling with the question, "Could God really love me?" My family's life experiences have been trying since Mia's birth, from financial turmoil experienced by so many in the 2008 economic downturn to raising a child with autism and epilepsy and the many complications that accompany this diagnosis. This Sunday morning, every concern seemed to stack high and have me questioning my value to anyone, let alone to God, whom I feared I let down in so many ways. And though I sat in church with my family and community, I felt alone in my struggle.

When the visiting speaker, Dr. Paul Conn, began his sermon, he asked the congregation a question along the lines of, "What is the hardest thing for you to believe in the Bible?" Dr. Conn went on to discuss some of the rather "unbelievable" miracles that took place in the Bible. I leaned over to my husband and whispered in his ear: "The hardest thing for me to believe is not that God made the world, parted the sea, or walked on water, but the hardest thing for me to believe is that God specifically loves me!"

In short order, this was exactly the "hardest thing to believe" that Dr. Conn highlighted for the congregation, and I was wowed as his sermon beautifully addressed the very issue with which I was wrestling. God is so good, so faithful, and so loving. Not only did I see that He loved me, but also that He loved me uniquely. No doubt many people needed to hear such a sermon, but God uniquely knew that I was asking this very question in my heart and He uniquely brought Dr. Conn and me together on that appointed day in that specific place so that I could receive, and he could deliver, this particular message from God.

When you are wondering how in the world the God of all creation could favor you, nothing breaks through the doubt like His Word.

Scripture is the perfect place to turn when we're feeling less than lovable. When you are wondering how in the world the God of all creation could favor you, nothing breaks through the doubt like His Word. Read the following verses and bask in His love.

We are each uniquely created by God.

> For you created my inmost being; you knit me together in my mother's womb. I praise you because I am fearfully and wonderfully made; your works are wonderful, I know that full well. My frame was not hidden from you when I was made in the secret place, when I was woven together in the depths of the earth. Your eyes saw my unformed body; all the days ordained for me were written in your book before one of them came to be.
>
> **Psalm 139:13-16**

> There are different kinds of gifts, but the same Spirit distributes them. There are different kinds of service, but the same Lord. There are different kinds of working, but in all of them and in everyone it is the same God at work. Now to each one the manifestation of the Spirit is given for the common good. To one there is given through the Spirit a message of wisdom, to another a message of knowledge by means of the same Spirit, to another faith by the same Spirit, to another gifts of healing by that one Spirit, to another miraculous powers, to another prophecy, to another distinguishing between spirits, to another speaking in different kinds of tongues, and to still another the interpretation of tongues. All these are the work of one and the same Spirit, and he distributes them to each one, just as he determines.
>
> **1 Corinthians 12:4-11**

We are each uniquely loved by God.

> Whoever has ears, let them hear what the Spirit says to the churches. To the one who is victorious, I will give some of the hidden manna. I will also give that person a white stone with a new name written on it, known only to the one who receives it.
>
> **Revelation 2:17**

If Christ gives you a unique name, known only between you and Christ, you can be sure there is a unique relationship and a unique love that go right along with it. Can you imagine even wanting to compare your name to that of anyone else's in the heavenly kingdom? This gift of relationship will be too sacred to inspire envy. It is hard to imagine a capacity to love so vast that it is able to love equally and uniquely. God's love is not a scarce commodity, and it does not need to be hoarded in order to remain with us. In fact, the more we share it, the more the understanding of His love grows inside of us.

If Christ gives you a unique name, known only between you and Christ you can be sure there is a unique relationship and a unique love that go right along with it.

So, how do we maintain our hope, our "beloved child of the King" awareness, when others seem to be succeeding in places we seem to be faltering? Do what John did. Start referring to yourself as "the disciple Jesus loves." Fill in the blank below with your name.

My name is _____ , the disciple Jesus loves.

It is powerful to speak the truth of Scripture!

3.5: Creating a Legacy

When we refer to ourselves as the beloved of Christ, we create a legacy. When my oldest daughter was around 10 years old, I found her in her room, snuggled up in her bed, surrounded by well-loved stuffed animals. Long past naptime age, it was curious to me that she seemed to be hiding there in the middle of the day. I asked her what she was up to and she responded, "Mommy, I love my room, my house. I feel safe here and sometimes I don't want to go out in the world. I just want to stay here forever."

But that little girl grew up and moved all the way across the country. What gave her the courage to leave the home she wanted to stay in forever? She had hope and faith! Hope for a great future, faith in the love we had for her, and the assurance that if life got rocky, she always has a place to call home. This gave her courage to face the unknown.

Our courage comes from our faith in the assurance of God's Spirit within us and all around us.

Our courage comes from our faith in the assurance of God's Spirit within us and all around us.

> What, then, shall we say in response to these things? If God is for us, who can be against us? He who did not spare his own Son, but gave him up for us all—how will he not also, along with him, graciously give us all things?
> **Romans 8:31-32**

God gives us power, love and self-control to act courageously in the face of our fears. He is with us and has prepared a place for us. And though we are all far from home, we can be deeply anchored in God's love even across the great divide.

Is your family legacy one of courage? Do you have personal testimonies of the courage you have in Christ to pass on to your children, family members, and community? Take a moment to write down one such story you have shared or might plan to share.

In pondering the role of courage while riding this often perilous and surprising ride, I have come to treasure the significance of passing a legacy of courage on to my children. The work in creating and maintaining a legacy involves being attentive to how we judge ourselves, particularly how we judge ourselves in relation to other parents we meet, or hear about, who are on this ride with us. As parents struggling with a unique challenge, we are prone to compare our own efforts to the efforts other parents are expending for their children.

I can tell you that I have had feelings of intimidation and awe over the distances other parents seem to be going for their child. I have read stories about parents who claim miraculous cures. Frankly, they overwhelm me. I have asked myself on more than one occasion, *Why can't I do all they have done? Am I somehow less capable, less worthy? Why am I not being led in the direction of a total cure for my child? Is God less responsive to me?*

In the worldly realm, I have been guilty of feeling "less than" when I compare myself to others. Yet with each passing year, I am continually reminded that such comparisons are meaningless. The people I most envy as having it all figured out, enjoying lives of ease, or possessing the magic cure for their child, always turn out to have ample trials and vulnerable points themselves. Jesus is clear on this saying, "In this world you will have trouble" (John 16:33). This passage in John goes on to say, "But take heart! I have overcome the world." Scripture assures us we have the power of God behind us. Our ability to overcome trial is firmly rooted in our decision to believe the truth of Scripture over the "easy way out roads" offered by the world.

Our ability to overcome trial is firmly rooted in our decision to believe the truth of Scripture over the "easy way out roads" offered by the world.

So, we must stand firm in our response to "super parent" stories. Let us be inspired by them, claim our identity as beloved children of the King, and ask what unique path of healing He has in store for our family. Scripture gives us many stories of great heroes. And these stories are not meant to intimidate us but rather to inspire us. In fact, in many cases, God includes the not-so-heroic details of the people involved in these stories. He wants us to see that they, like us, have flaws and fears. Scripture relates Noah's drunkenness, Jacob's deceit, Joseph's boasting, Samson's womanizing, David's adultery and murder, Peter's denial, and Paul's persecution of Christ's followers. Clearly in their moments of corruption, these heroes are not attending to the Spirit of God. But when they do acknowledge God's Spirit, the result is courage and power to do amazing things. This courage and power is also available to us, because God's Spirit is within us.

The stories below demonstrate the power of faith in the face of impossibly frightening circumstances. Take a minute to read these familiar stories of courage from Scripture:

- **Daniel in the Lions' Den: Daniel 6:1-23**

- **The Fiery Furnace: Daniel 3:1-30**

Consider keeping a record of your own stories of courage. The only ingredient you need to get started is faith. You know just how and from whom you get that precious gift!

Look for the opportunity to hold a special celebration either just between you and God or with your family and/or friends. Celebrate something you or someone you know has courageously overcome in His name.

Small Group Discussion

Study Three - God Gives Us a Spirit of Courage

After you have individually reviewed the readings and reflection questions, meet with your small group using the suggested format below:

Believe: We believe God gives us a spirit of courage!

Scripture Reading: What do these verses mean to you?

> May the God of hope fill you with all joy and peace as you trust in him,
> so that you may overflow with hope by the power of the Holy Spirit.
> **Romans 15:13**

> Who shall separate us from the love of Christ? Shall trouble or hardship or persecution or famine or nakedness or danger or sword? As it is written: "For your sake we face death all day long; we are considered as sheep to be slaughtered." No, in all these things we are more than conquerors through him who loved us. For I am convinced that neither death nor life, neither angels nor demons, neither the present nor the future, nor any powers, neither height nor depth, nor anything else in all creation, will be able to separate us from the love of God that is in Christ Jesus our Lord.
> **Romans 8:35-39**

Engage: Review the questions below and allow each person to participate in the discussion.

3.1
- **(1) How does fear prevent you from experiencing God in any area of your life?**
- **(2) What do you do, or where do you turn, when you are afraid?**

3.2
- **(3) What is your personal definition of faith?**
- **(4) How does your faith compare in size to a mustard seed?**
- **(5) How have you experienced the God-given Spirit of courage in a tough situation?**

3.3
- **(6) What keeps you going when you must do without things you define as needed in life?**
- **(7) What things of substance in your life demonstrate hopes fulfilled?**

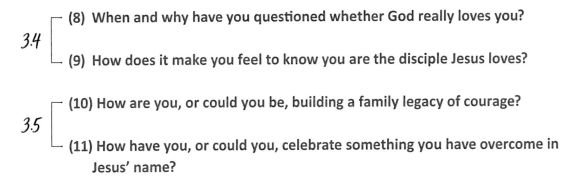

3.4
(8) When and why have you questioned whether God really loves you?

(9) How does it make you feel to know you are the disciple Jesus loves?

3.5
(10) How are you, or could you be, building a family legacy of courage?

(11) How have you, or could you, celebrate something you have overcome in Jesus' name?

Celebrate: Give praise for the growth of our faith, the hope and evidence we have in Christ, the privilege of being uniquely loved and the opportunity to create a legacy of courage for our loved ones.

Pray: *May each of our families be strengthened in courage and grow ever more cognizant of God's presence. Knowing we are worthy of love as children of the King, may it be said of us, as Paul wrote in his second letter to the Thessalonians, "Your faith is growing more and more, and the love all of you have for one another is increasing" (1:3). Amen.*

(Add the prayer intentions of group members.)

Trust in the LORD with all your heart,
lean not on your own understanding;
in all your ways submit to him,
and he will make your paths straight.
Proverbs 3:5-6

STUDY FOUR
GOD SHOWS US THE WAY

Commit to Follow the Track

We are always moving in life, always trying to get to another place from the place we currently find ourselves. And in order to move from one place to another, we need a track to follow. As you heard in "Categorical Panoply," the dilemma for parents of special needs children is not that there is no path, but that there are so many! So far in working with Mia, we have used ABA, OT, PT, speech, sensory integration, music therapy, oxygen chambers, supplements, HANDLE, homeopathy, kinesiology, pharmaceuticals, Floortime, Son-Rise, and special diets. But, ultimately, what has proven the most beneficial is lots of prayerful conversation with God.

The Bible tells us to trust and acknowledge the superior wisdom of God, so that He can direct our paths.

> Walk in obedience to all that the LORD your God has commanded you, so that you
> may live and prosper and prolong your days in the land that you will possess.
> **Deuteronomy 5:33**

Deuteronomy 5:33 is a beautiful verse, yet when I first considered it for this study, I found myself saying, "But Lord, so much has not gone well with me, nor for my Mia." But then God brought a verse in 2 Corinthians to mind: "For we live by faith, not by sight" (2 Corinthians 5:7).

By the world's standards of a successful, desirable life path, mine has gone quite astray and much seems to have turned out all wrong. Yet for me, it is these very "wrongs" that drive me so fully into God's presence. I have learned it is not what is happening in my life that determines my capability to move forward. Rather, the circumstances of my life are like landmarks along the route I travel—their importance, their meaning, and their consequences are all shaped by my God who is my traveling companion. With God as my guide, I can adapt to all the twists and turns and experience a sense of purpose.

> Show me your ways, LORD, teach me your paths.
> Guide me in your truth and teach me,
> for you are God my Savior,
> and my hope is in you all day long.
> **Psalm 25:4-5**

If you have one or more people in your life who have been with you through thick and thin, you have experienced the beauty of a traveling companion in the flesh. When that relationship is forged on God's principals, the depth of what you experience together blossoms into meaningful purpose for each of you, as well as those around you. I have heard it said you can tell much about a person by the five people closest to them. Who better to choose as number one than God, and then trust Him to name the other four and more!

I need to stay in close contact with God's guidance for my life to walk this special-needs path. In fact, so much of the time I need Him to supernaturally lift me out from under the weight, both real and imagined, of my burdens, so that I can take that first step. If God says walking in His commands is my path to all going well, then I just need to believe it. I need to walk it in faith even if worldly sight deceives me. I need to choose to believe Him when He says He can use all things for good.

Study Four – God Shows Us the Way

4.1: Study the Path

Just as we carefully research and implement a chosen therapy to reach our child, it is important to carefully study God's plan to reach us. After all, the entire Bible is the story of His desire to lead humanity back into a blissful "walking and talking in the Garden of Eden" type of relationship with Him. Studying the Word and engaging in prayerful conversations with God offer us vehicles to receive God's profoundly wise guidance for our lives.

Studying the Word and engaging in prayerful conversations with God offer us vehicles to receive God's profoundly wise guidance for our lives.

Scripture itself has much to say about studying the Word. Take a moment to look up, write out, and reflect upon these passages:

Joshua 1:8

2 Timothy 3:16-17

Acts 17:11

This is our second look at Acts 17:11, for just like the Berean Jews in this passage, receiving the Word with eagerness will tremendously benefit our lives. As we study it, meditate on it, and speak it over our lives and over our children, we can be assured that the Word is worthy of our full confidence. Any therapy path we choose has its pros and cons. Some therapies may work for your child, others seem useless or even cause regression, but God's path comes with a foolproof guarantee.

Read the passages below and note God's 100 percent guarantee.

So is my word that goes out from my mouth: It will not return
to me empty, but will accomplish what I desire and
achieve the purpose for which I sent it.
Isaiah 55:11

Let us then approach God's throne of grace with confidence, so that we
may receive mercy and find grace to help us in our time of need.
Hebrews 4:16

This is the confidence we have in approaching God: that if we ask anything
according to his will, he hears us. And if we know that he hears us—
whatever we ask—we know that we have what we asked of him.
1 John 5:14-15

As parents of special needs children, we often find our chosen therapy paths
fail to cure or assist our children. Perhaps we can take some guidance from
this story about Thomas Edison inventing the light bulb. He tried over 2,000
experiments before he got it right. A young reporter asked him how he felt after
failing so many times. He said, "I never failed once. I invented the light bulb. It just
happened to be a 2,000-step process."

When I have attended special-needs conferences, parents have told me stories
about kicking themselves for wasting money and spending time on useless, or
even regressive, therapies. But wouldn't it be more useful for us to pat ourselves
on the back for trying something, and then give ourselves credit for realizing it
was not working so that we can move toward the right solution in our own 2,000-
step process? Let's speak with confidence and say, "I haven't failed; I am moving
along toward the solution."

**What therapies or strategies are you using with your child or in
your family life that you are questioning?**

Write out your specific concerns regarding every therapy or strategy you are considering or questioning.

Moving ever closer to God is its own 2,000-step process—one I have learned to enjoy immensely. Scripture—the powerful praying of the Word—and Christ's indwelling Spirit keep me in ever closer communion with God. My personal experiences with God are my solid proof that God is interested in every detail of my life, including what therapies I choose for my child and how we come together as a family and community around her.

If you are experiencing doubts about a current therapy decision, ask God to reveal if this hesitation, or "not working" issue, is an ungodly roadblock trying to get you to quit when you are so close to victory or a signpost from God to turn in another direction.

Dear friends, do not believe every spirit, but test the spirits to see whether they are from God, because many false prophets have gone out into the world.
1 John 4:1

...test the spirits to see whether they are from God...
1 John 4:1

Let God guide your path. Let Him work with your strengths despite what you may consider are your limitations in terms of your given resources of money, skill set, time, support people, and many other factors. He is a God of impossible outcomes. You can trust Him with your life.

4.2: The Narrow Gate

Have you heard it said that the end justifies the means? Not so in God's economy. God is all about the means, because He is designed to be the end. God's means involve walking through a narrow gate.

Enter through the narrow gate. For wide is the gate
and broad is the road that leads to destruction, and
many enter through it. But small is the gate and narrow
the road that leads to life, and only a few find it.
Matthew 7:13-14

We will explore the narrow gate referenced above later in this study. For today, I think it will be helpful to examine some of the worldly gates we walk through as the parent of a special needs child. One of the gates my family opened in our search to heal Mia led us to a program called Son-Rise. Part of the Son-Rise philosophy involves concentration on the quality of the therapist's proactive interaction with the child despite the child's response. In other words, when working with a child who has little-to-no desire for social acceptability, it is important not to take the child's response to your efforts personally. Most of the time, the child neither understands the concept of hurting your feelings nor the concept of appropriate social interaction.

Early in our therapy program, I remember checking in on a session in progress and finding the therapist in tears while Mia stoically pounded on her. I asked one of my older daughters to take over the session and sat down with the crying therapist to find out what had so upset her. Every therapist in our program knew, and was prepared for, the fact that Mia sometimes hit. This sweet woman explained to me that she loved my daughter so much, had been so excited to spend time with her, and was so looking forward to a breakthrough that Mia's violent attack had overwhelmed her with sorrow. She became so focused on Mia's reactions that she lost sight of the objectives we had discussed at our last meeting. She lost sight of the roadmap we had laid out to proactively deal with Mia's violent outbursts. She lost her way because she focused on what she wanted from Mia instead of focusing on what she was providing for Mia.

We sometimes focus so singularly on what we want from everyone and everything we lose sight of the gate to well-being outlined for us by God. That gate revolves around our acceptance of Jesus Christ as the one and only Savior.

Don't we just do this all the time? We focus so much on what we want from life and people that we let circumstances and the responses of others drive our actions. In fact, we sometimes focus so singularly on what we want from everyone and everything we lose sight of the gate to well-being outlined for us by God. That gate revolves around our acceptance of Jesus Christ as the one and only Savior. Accepting Christ is the means to living a proactive, rather than a reactive, life.

> **Note if there is any area of your life where you have been focused on the end without regard for the means?**

I am confident that every parent reading this study has good intent to do the best you can for your children and your family, and you each strive to improve whenever something is not working. We want to find the best education, best therapy, best teachers, best food, best medicines, and best parenting methods for our children. But honestly, sometimes the best we fleshly mortals can do involves lots of tears and the desperate need for a day off. Be merciful to yourselves, as God is merciful to you. Be prepared to make mistakes through both intentional and unintentional actions. Don't beat yourself up, but rather turn back to God and begin again, and when you once again fail, turn back to God and begin again, over and over and over. It is the cyclical nature of the God-man interaction that our failures continually drive us back to God.

Be merciful to yourselves, as God is merciful to you.

> **Consider the counsel of James to the twelve tribes of Israel, then answer the question which follows.**

> James, a servant of God and of the Lord Jesus Christ,
> To the twelve tribes scattered among the nations: Greetings.
> Consider it pure joy, my brothers and sisters, whenever you face
> trials of many kinds, because you know that the testing of your
> faith produces perseverance. Let perseverance finish its work so that
> you may be mature and complete, not lacking anything. If any of
> you lacks wisdom, you should ask God, who gives generously
> to all without finding fault, and it will be given to you.
> **James 1:1-5**

As part of our quest for wisdom from God, ask yourself if it really is your responsibility to fix your child, or does God have another end goal in mind for you? Consider how much you are involving God in the means to attaining your goals. Write your thoughts below.

It is the world's very brokenness that deeply reminds us how much we need a Savior.

Clearly, we all want our children to be completely healed. We want this for our children, for ourselves, for our families. We want to alleviate the trials of raising a very care-intensive human being. However, achieving our definition of a cure within our time frame is not 100 percent up to us. We live in a broken world, but while living in this broken world, we also have the choice to offer healing, to bring the Band-Aids and attempt to repair, to the extent we can, what's broken. So, we do our good work with God's Spirit and Word as our guide and we also allow others a chance to be healers and offer their aid. It is the world's very brokenness that deeply reminds us how much we need a Savior. Accepting our need for Christ is entering into the narrow gate. God will use all things to remind us of this, and He does so for our eternal good.

Look up Ephesians 2:10 and write this Scripture out below. How can you personalize this Word to your life?

Ask God to lead you in all the good works He has prepared for you!

4.3: Good Intent = God Intent

Remember the story about Mia and the toy throwing as related in section 2.5? My first reaction was far from one of my best parenting moments, but even if I, in a moment of fleshly weakness, considered taking the wrong path, God stepped in. Rather than letting me resort to the same unproductive behavior as my child, He had a better work in store for me. He had a higher calling on my life.

Make a list of your typical weekly "to-do" items below.

My list includes things that fall under work, family, social, and spiritual responsibilities. It is a long list, and I do not always approach each to-do with the best frame of mind. I admit sometimes I feel rather overwhelmed or put upon to complete some of my to-dos, but I generally tackle all of them with good intent. However, as my walk with God has grown, I find myself questioning my definition of good intent. It is one thing to say I meant to "do good"; it is another thing entirely to say I actually "did good."

So, in order to move farther from "meant to do good" and closer to "did good," I began to see that if I really wanted to walk through life with **good intent,** I needed to do it with **God intent.**

> **Consider the equation "Good Intent = God Intent" and note ways you might apply this equation to a current difficult situation in your life.**

Part of the problem, often noted in Scripture, is that all the people were doing as they saw "fit in their own eyes." There was no common definition of "doing the right thing," and they had completely forgotten, or were ignoring, God-given guidance about what doing the right thing entailed.

> **Look up the following Scripture and write it out below:**
>
> **Judges 17:6**

Only following God's ways can ensure the right we do is right for all concerned. When we equate good intent to God intent, we have a meaningful definition on which to base our words and actions.

This verse is repeated in Judges 21:25. Between these two verses is the story of God's people engaging in traitorous, murderous, and sorrowful ways. What was right in each person's eyes did not take into account what was right in God's eyes. Only following God's ways can ensure the right we do is right for all concerned. When we equate good intent to God intent, we have a meaningful definition on which to base our words and actions. No other definition of good intent can hit the mark every time.

> Take another look at your weekly "to-do" list and consider if there are "to-dos" that need to change, disappear, or be added. Rewrite them in a way that reflects the good God calls you to do.

4.4: God's Path Is Paved With Love

God is clear when He exhorts us again and again to walk in His ways. He is clear that the real path is love. The truth for me is that no matter how sad, how hard, how unfair I feel Mia's situation is, nor how crazy Mia's situation drives me, I have been called to be crazy in love with my child. I thank God for His mastery of design in bringing Mia into my life as an adorable bundle of "sweet smelling babiness." She won my heart as He intended.

> Look up Colossians 3:12-15 and write it below:

When we put on love, Scripture opens to us in the Spirit of joyous revelation. God's Spirit guides us to the real track to follow—our choice to love God and love others, our choice to give ourselves over to God's intent for every choice and interaction in our lives, and our choice to "Do everything in love" (1 Corinthians 16:14). We are called to practice this with our children, especially when they are behaving in an unlovely manner—this is when we most need to see God's face and choose love.

> As a prisoner for the Lord, then, I urge you to live a life worthy
> of the calling you have received. Be completely humble and gentle;
> be patient, bearing with one another in love. Make every effort to
> keep the unity of the Spirit through the bond of peace.
> **Ephesians 4:1-3**

When we walk with God, He empowers us to love our children, to offer dedication and service to them. That is our real responsibility to them—not to fix, but to love our children. It's crazy; it makes no sense. They can take so much out of us. Sometimes, they are so hard to love, but we can still choose to love them with the power of the Holy Spirit. This applies to everyone in our lives and we need to apply it with the utmost steadfastness to those who are intimately helping us raise our special needs child.

Sometimes, they are so hard to love, but we can still choose to love them with the power of the Holy Spirit.

Perhaps God is calling you to reevaluate your walk of love. If there is anything He is calling you to do to walk in His love in word and deed, ask Him to reveal it to you and write what comes to mind in the space below.

4.5: No More Hiding

Genesis 3:8 tells us that Adam and Eve "heard the sound of the LORD God as he was walking in the garden in the cool of the day, and they hid from the LORD God among the trees of the garden" (KJV). They hid from Him because they were ashamed. God had provided guidance for their behaviors and they had acted in a manner contrary to His guidance. They could do this because God gave them free will to make their own decisions about whether they would follow His guidance or not. Because we have the gift of free will, we too can each choose to block off all, or part, of our lives from God.

I have a very vivid remembrance of a day I momentarily hid from the Lord. Thankfully, in a monumentally attention-grabbing way, He called my gaze right back where it belonged—eyes upward on Him. I had just picked up Mia from elementary school where the principal had sternly reprimanded me—in lieu of Mia—because Mia had once again pulled the fire alarm, causing all the typical chaos such a situation entails. I was already having one of those emotionally draining "poor pitiful parent of a special needs child" kind of day, and her lambasting was the straw that broke the camel's back. As I drove away from the school, my focus was on the self-pity and shame I was feeling when it definitely needed to be elsewhere. As I learned at the next traffic light, my focus should have been both an earthly, and a heavenly, elsewhere!

At the stoplight, I lay hunched over the steering wheel in anguished self-absorption until I heard the driver next to me honk his horn. I looked over to see the man in the driver's seat gesturing upward and back with a disapproving look on his face. I glanced up and then back and discovered to my horror that Mia was not buckled in her seat, her car window was open, and she was gone!

I jumped out of the car to see Mia dancing around contentedly on top of the van. Fortunately, a friend, who also happens to have a special needs child, was the driver of the car behind me. She rushed out of her car to help me coax the oblivious Mia off the car roof. Another woman who identified herself as a caregiver from a nearby nursing home also jumped out of her car to assist us. As my eyes focused upward on Mia, they were consequently drawn upward toward heaven—just as God would have it! I took the hint as I climbed on top of the van to hand a happy-go-lucky Mia down to my friend's open arms.

My friend followed me the short way home, and we had a good tear-soaked laugh in my driveway. The memory makes me laugh to this day and I never forgot to lock the car windows again. You see, rule number one when driving with Mia was to lock down the window controls because she was prone to throwing her shoes out the window and climbing around the car. Clearly, I had neglected to attend to this important detail in favor of focusing on something totally beyond my control.

But God knew what was going on with Mia, even if I was too lost in my own misery to see it. He also knew just how to use it to get my attention. I love His humor. I love His lessons. I love how He is with me in every moment. And most important, rather than hide in any useless pit of sorrow and shame, I want to stay in His Word faithfully enough to hear the prompting of the Holy Spirit, in my "far too fast to forget" heart, to run toward God in every situation.

> **Is there a time or area of your life you have hidden or are hiding from God? Look up Micah 6:8 and write in your own words what it says to you.**

God's guidelines are the only path to getting what we really want. He offers peace, joy, relationship fulfillment, and a home of abundance with Him. Sometimes, we don't even realize we are hiding from Him. We get so consumed with our own goings on that we forget He is right there with us through it all.

God's guidelines are the only path to getting what we really want. He offers peace, joy, relationship fulfillment, and a home of abundance with Him.

> For you were once darkness, but now you are light
> in the Lord. Live as children of light.
> **Ephesians 5:8**

> As for God, his way is perfect: The LORD's word is flawless;
> he shields all who take refuge in him. For who is God besides the LORD?
> And who is the Rock except our God? It is God who arms me with
> strength and keeps my way secure. He makes my feet like the feet of a
> deer; he causes me to stand on the heights. He trains my hands for battle;
> my arms can bend a bow of bronze. You make your saving help my shield,
> and your right hand sustains me; your help has made me great. You
> provide a broad path for my feet, so that my ankles do not give way.
> **Psalm 18:30-36**

Scripture tells us walking with God, as opposed to hiding from Him, is the light-giving way. But how do we gain access to a place we can walk with God? Let's

Entering a narrow gate to find a field of possibilities is God's specialty — all things are possible with God.

consider the portion of Matthew 7 we reviewed in the reading for 4.2. Verse 13 calls us to enter "by the narrow gate." In John 10:9, Christ tells us He is that gate, saying, "I am the gate; whoever enters through me will be saved. They will come in and go out, and find pasture." He also tells us in perfect harmony with Psalm 18, that once we come in the gate, we will find a "pasture," which can certainly be categorized as a "broad path." Entering a narrow gate to find a field of possibilities is God's specialty—all things are possible with God.

Read the two verses below and ask God to reveal to you how both statements can be true.

Small is the gate and narrow the road
that leads to life, and only a few find it.
Matthew 7:14

You provide a broad path for my feet,
so that my ankles do not give way.
Psalm 18:36

Now ask God to open the small gate and widen the narrow path into a broad pasture for your feet. Be ready for an amazing walk through God's garden of grace, walking humbly by His side as a child of His light.

Small Group Discussion

Study Four - God Shows Us the Way

After you have individually reviewed the readings and reflection questions, meet with your small group using the suggested format below:

Believe: We believe God's path is the only path worth walking!

Scripture Reading: What do these verses mean to you?

> The LORD makes firm the steps of the one who delights in him;
> though he may stumble, he will not fall,
> for the LORD upholds him with his hand.
> **Psalm 37:23-24**

> You make known to me the path of life;
> you will fill me with joy in your presence,
> with eternal pleasures at your right hand.
> **Psalm 16:11**

Engage: Review the questions below and allow each person to participate in the discussion.

4.1

(1) What does Scripture tell us about studying Scripture?

(2) What is God's 100 percent guarantee about the Scripture's purpose?

(3) Are there any strategies you are using with your child that you are questioning?

(4) Has prayer been helpful in choosing strategies for your child?

4.2

(5) Are there areas of your life where you have been focused on the end without regard for the means?

(6) Do you think it is your responsibility to fix your child?

(7) How much do you regularly involve God in caring for your child?

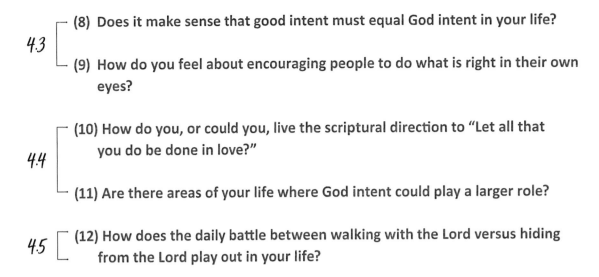

4.3

(8) Does it make sense that good intent must equal God intent in your life?

(9) How do you feel about encouraging people to do what is right in their own eyes?

4.4

(10) How do you, or could you, live the scriptural direction to "Let all that you do be done in love?"

(11) Are there areas of your life where God intent could play a larger role?

4.5

(12) How does the daily battle between walking with the Lord versus hiding from the Lord play out in your life?

Celebrate: We are blessed by the great availability of the Word and opportunities to study it in this wonderful country. Celebrate Christ for being the narrow gate that leads us to God's broad path and plentiful pasture.

Pray: Thank You for Your Word, and grant us a great thirst to study it and meditate on it. We accept Christ as our Savior and want to walk humbly with God, for we are convinced that truly good intent equals God intent. You have paved Your way with love, and there is no part of our lives that You do not see. Help us follow You and miraculously broaden our paths to bounteous pastures. Amen.

(Add any group members' prayer intentions.)

Trust him at all times, you people;
pour out your hearts to him,
for God is our refuge.
Psalm 62:8

You Can Let It All Out With God

Experience the Freedom to SCREAM!

When we are facing trials, we need to know it is okay to groan, scream, be afraid, and even feel like we cannot live out the circumstances of our lives another second! Acknowledging that we feel "hopeless" is an essential truth, because we were not designed to do this on our own. We were designed to walk with God, to lean on His wisdom, His strength, His compassion.

God is our best sounding board. God wants us to pour out our hearts to Him. He is always listening. In fact, as we discussed in Study Two, God knows the words we speak before we speak them. Psalm 139:4 attests to this, "Before a word is on my tongue you, LORD, know it completely."

God even understands our speechlessness and gives us the Holy Spirit to interpret our groaning. "In the same way, the Spirit helps us in our weakness. We do not know what we ought to pray for, but the Spirit himself intercedes for us through wordless groans" (Romans 8:26). The ESV paints a different poetic picture saying the Spirit intercedes, "with groanings too deep for words." Isn't it comforting to know the Holy Spirit prays on our behalf when we are beyond words?

The Psalms are wonderful biblical examples of pouring out the human heart to God. A large number of the Psalms are attributed to David. In Acts 13:22, Paul spoke of God testifying that David was "a man after His own heart." In all of David's tribulation and glory, the Psalms depict him before God pouring out his distress or elation. No matter the circumstances of your emotional state, the Book of Psalms is sure to contain within its pages words that mirror your heart's condition and help you share it with the Lord.

> Have mercy on me, LORD, for I am faint; heal me, LORD, for my bones are in agony.
> My soul is in deep anguish. How long, LORD, how long? Turn, LORD, and deliver me;
> save me because of your unfailing love. Among the dead no one proclaims your name.
> Who praises you from the grave? I am worn out from my groaning.
> All night long I flood my bed with weeping and drench my couch with tears.
> My eyes grow weak with sorrow; they fail because of all my foes.
> **Psalm 6:1-7**

Too numerous to count are the times I have just as desperately cried out to God. My choked sobs have detailed my sorrows, complaints, and fears, or my pleadings for healing, peace, joy, provision, or my entreaties for Him to come near and lift me out of the pit. Praise the Lord that Jesus died to do this very thing—to lift us out of every hellish pit. Count on the sacrifice of Jesus to give you strength when your knees buckle with sorrow and your frame caves in with grief. Let us say to Jesus, like Simon Peter who, when Jesus asked the Twelve apostles if they wanted to desert Him like so many others, replied, "Lord, to whom shall we go to? You have the words of eternal life. We have come to believe and know that you are the Holy One of God" (John 6:68-69).

Study Five – You Can Let It All Out With God

5.1: God Consoles and Gives Rest

How comforting it is to share your emotional tribulation with others. A good confidant will console you, offer action to assist you, and point your state of mind in the right direction. I spoke at a support group for parents of children with autism a number of years ago, and it just so happened that the audience was composed largely of fathers. When we started talking about our emotional states, one father spoke with particularly poignant words saying, "I've always gone into my boys' rooms before I retire for the evening and put my hands on their back, to see that they are breathing. Since the time my oldest was diagnosed, I sometimes think to myself, as I cross the threshold to his room: *Maybe he won't be breathing and maybe that would be okay.*"

This father had not confessed his frightening thoughts to anyone before this night. But he so needed to tell someone. And he needed to hear that he was not a monster for having such thoughts. So many of us share them, wondering at times if the "here after" might be better than the "here now" for us, our families, and our child. In sharing his feelings with us, he set others free to share their own hidden, and often self-incriminating, thoughts. It was a powerful moment for all the men in that room, and a powerful moment for me.

Perhaps, you, like me, grew up under the tutelage that if you had nothing nice to say, you should say nothing at all. However, the truth is, sometimes, as in the story above, the unlovely emotions we feel should be shared with others, and always they should be shared with God! Everything in life is meant to point us to God, from gratefulness in abundance to gut-wrenching anguish in difficulty. God's ears are always open and ever yearning to hear from us.

The unlovely emotions we feel should always be shared with God! Everything in life is meant to point us to God, from gratefulness in abundance to gut-wrenching anguish in difficulty. God's ears are always open and ever yearning to hear from us.

In a moment of deep despair, David penned these inspired words, "Be merciful to me, LORD, for I am in distress; my eyes grow weak with sorrow, my soul and body with grief. My life is consumed by anguish and my years by groaning; my strength fails because of my affliction, and my bones grow weak" (Psalm 31:9-10).

Can you relate to the distress expressed by David above?

If there is a burden on your heart, take a moment to pour it out to the Lord. He longs to share, and lighten, your burdens.

Come to me, all you who are weary and burdened, and I will give you rest.
Matthew 11:28

Depression, 'woe is me' feelings, fear, doubt, weakness, financial stress, thoughts of abandonment, and loneliness are some of the many foes we face in raising a child with special needs. I pray you will take refuge in the Father through Christ. In Matthew 11:28, Jesus invites us to come to Him saying, "Come to me, all you who are weary and burdened, and I will give you rest."

Look up the following verses and write them out in your own words:

Psalm 10:17

Psalm 17:6-8

God desires to be our refuge. Take a moment to thank Him for listening, loving, and rescuing us.

5.2: God Hears and Heals

God is our creator. He gave us the capacity to feel, and He delights when we share those feelings with Him. Psalm 46:1 tells us that God is our "ever present help" in time of need. He is always available to us, night or day.

We are always invited to acknowledge our emotional state before God, even when it is less than glamorous because God's presence is an interactive one. When we come before Him in earnest, His response is always one of healing. Scripture assures us of this.

Look up the following verses and write out the portions surrounding any derivative of the word "heal."

Exodus 15:26

Psalm 107:20

Acts 10:38

1 Peter 2:24

God knows the form of healing we each need. Sometimes what we have in mind, in terms of the healing we need, may not match up with what God knows is best. We can guard against thoughts that stray from God's wisdom by taking all thoughts captive to Christ.

> We demolish arguments and every pretension that sets
> itself up against the knowledge of God, and we take captive
> every thought to make it obedient to Christ.
> **2 Corinthians 10:5**

Because we are assured of complete healing in our eternal life with God, we can rest assured that everything God does for and with us here is all part of the preparatory stages toward our final healing. Sometimes a miraculous healing comes our way quickly, other times it may feel something like pre-op testing,

God knows the form of healing we each need.

How sweet are your words to my taste, sweeter than honey to my mouth! Psalm 119:103

painful but necessary to get down to the root cause of our illness and reveal the cure. There have been many times in my life when I have choked down bitter pills, hard medicine, to bring about the healing I needed. Remember the famous musical lines for the classic movie, Mary Poppins: "A spoonful of sugar helps the medicine go down." My spoonful of sugar is God's Word. God tells us we do "not live by bread alone, but on every word that comes from the mouth of God" (Matthew 4:4). His promises and assurances are what make the hard times bearable, and yes, even sweet. The psalmist said, "How sweet are your words to my taste, sweeter than honey to my mouth!" (Psalm 119:103).

If there are bitter situations in your life that need the sweetness of God's Word, take a moment to jot these down and perhaps look up other Scripture references applying to your circumstances. Then pray for God's healing touch.

5.3: God Calls Us to Relationship and Community

Supporting others can be among the most constructive uses for the outpouring of our emotions. In fact, God calls us to community specifically to support one another.

We all have less than saintly reactions to difficult situations in our lives and certainly to the news that our child is compromised in some way. The needs and behaviors that accompany a special-needs diagnosis can be extremely taxing on parents and families. The willingness of the father, whose story you read in 5.1, to acknowledge his emotions gave the entire group a forum for understanding the purpose of all our varied sentiments and finding constructive use for them. Supporting others can be among the most constructive uses for the outpouring of our emotions. In fact, God calls us to community specifically to support one another. When believers gather together at the foot of the cross and the throne room of God, there is no better, and no safer, place to express ourselves and help us make sense of the way we feel.

**Have you found comfort or inspiration in a story or personal experience someone shared with you recently?
If so, relate the story below.**

As a participant and speaker at countless special needs discussions and conferences, I have witnessed that no matter how much emotional strain we experience, some parents continue to be the best mothers and fathers they know how to be, while others are crushed under the weight of their emotional state. Statistics say close to 50 percent of mothers raising children with special needs suffer severe depression. And fathers are cited to become distant or absent due to feelings of powerlessness to keep up with the financial and emotional demands of fathering a special needs child. It can certainly be fatiguing to march through a daily routine of therapies, medications, and behavioral challenges. We often feel we must arrange our daily schedules exclusively to "fix" our child. From special meals, to medications, to therapy schedules, no wonder the midnight hour comes complete with mother meltdown and father fatigue syndrome.

The truth is, we are going to face heightened emotional ups and downs in raising our special needs children. In order to survive those devastating lows, it is important to have constructive places to turn—places we know build us up, give us courage, and give us joy. The world offers us many places to turn with our sorrows—from blaming others, wearing a chip on our shoulders, living cut off from others or angry at the world and God, to finding escape in drinking, drugs, or abandoning our families for a life we imagine will be less stressful.

Making good choices about what to do with our difficult emotions requires clear-headed thinking and wisdom. When we are in the throes of crisis, these two essential ingredients are often in short supply. But unlike our fleeting wisdom, God's wisdom is infinite and unchanging.

How blessed are we to have a Father whose willingness and abilities are so great on our behalves as to be immeasurable!

We looked at Ephesians 3:20 in the NKJV in 2.3 of Study Two as assurance of what God can do when we commit ourselves and our emotions to Him. Let's look at it again in the NIV where the translation says He can do "immeasurably more than all we ask or imagine" (Ephesians 3:20). How blessed are we to have a Father whose willingness and abilities are so great on our behalves as to be immeasurable!

Take a moment to read Psalm 40:1-13 and be encouraged.

I waited patiently for the LORD;
he turned to me and heard my cry.
He lifted me out of the slimy pit,
out of the mud and mire;
he set my feet on a rock
and gave me a firm place to stand.
He put a new song in my mouth,
a hymn of praise to our God.
Many will see and fear the LORD
and put their trust in him.
Blessed is the one
who trusts in the LORD,
who does not look to the proud,
to those who turn aside to false gods.
Many, LORD my God,
are the wonders you have done,
the things you planned for us.
None can compare with you;
were I to speak and tell of your deeds,
they would be too many to declare.
Sacrifice and offering you did not desire—
but my ears you have opened—
burnt offerings and sin offerings you did not require.
Then I said, "Here I am, I have come—
it is written about me in the scroll.
I desire to do your will, my God;
your law is within my heart."
I proclaim your saving acts in the great assembly;
I do not seal my lips, LORD,
as you know.
I do not hide your righteousness in my heart;

I speak of your faithfulness and your saving help.
I do not conceal your love and your faithfulness
from the great assembly.
Do not withhold your mercy from me, LORD;
may your love and faithfulness always protect me.
For troubles without number surround me;
my sins have overtaken me, and I cannot see.
They are more than the hairs of my head,
and my heart fails within me.
Be pleased to save me, LORD;
come quickly, LORD, to help me.

5.4: Stones of Remembrance

Hundreds of emotionally charged moments have been etched into my very being in raising Mia. The screams and tears issued in my battle to parent Mia have, each and every time, brought me to the throne of grace with a heart ripped open wide. The incredible moments of angst smoothed over by the even more incredible response of my Father in heaven, are my firmest anchors to faith. They are stones in my tower of remembrance.

Scripture records time and time again stories of God's people calling out for His intercession. He always answered them in His perfect timing! And He does so in the most amazing and unexpected ways. One of my favorite biblical intercessions is the miraculous crossing of the Jordan River.

Joshua 3:15, states the condition of the Jordan at the time the Israelites crossed as "flood stage." A bit of research suggests that the Jordan is 40 feet wide at its widest, but during flood stage it can get to 1 mile wide and 150 feet deep. Let that sink in, because this was no babbling brook or sunlit stream they were told to cross, this was a seriously raging river. The only way for the Israelites to cross this river was with God's help. Don't miss that important point.

I am reminded of a book I loved reading with my children when they were younger. The book, *We're Going on a Bear Hunt,* is written by Michael Rosen and has whimsical illustrations by Helen Oxenbury. I love this book because it speaks of the importance of sticking together as a family. The chorus repeats after every situation the family finds themselves in on this journey: "We can't go over it. We can't go under it. Oh no! We've got to go through it!" I can just imagine the Israelites uttering this very same phrase!

If God asks you to go through it, you can be assured He will bring you out on the other side. Take a moment to reflect on a time God has asked you to go through a seemingly impossible situation and write about how He brought you through it below.

Joshua 3:15-16 goes on to say, "As soon as the priests who carried the ark reached the Jordan and their feet touched the water's edge, the water from upstream stopped flowing. It piled up in a heap a great distance away, at a town called Adam in the vicinity of Zarethan, while the water flowing down to the Sea of the Arabah (that is, the Dead Sea) was completely cut off."

God is always a faithful Word keeper.

Make note of the words, "a great distance away." This meant that God stopped the river many miles upstream. If we consider the flow rate of the river, the priest may have needed to stand there for some time, perhaps several hours, before the water stopped flowing. It must have crossed their mind once or twice that Joshua might have gotten the message a bit wrong. They may have wondered if God was going to show up at all. But Joshua was a faithful Word bearer and God is always a faithful Word keeper. The river did dry up. The Israelites walked across DRY ground, not moist ground, but totally DRY ground. Amazing!

Are there times you feel you have had a promise from God to do a particular thing in your life, yet it has seemed like He took a very long time indeed to show up? What helped you wait faithfully? When He did show up, how did you feel?

Once the people were across, but before the priests carrying the ark stepped out of the riverbed, God commanded Joshua to send one man from each of the 12 tribes back into the middle of the riverbed.

> Each of you is to take up a stone on his shoulder, according to the number of the tribes of the Israelites, to serve as a sign among you. In the future, when your children ask you, 'What do these stones mean?' tell them that the flow of the Jordan was cut off before the ark of the covenant of the LORD. When it crossed the Jordan, the waters of the Jordan were cut off. These stones are to be a memorial to the people of Israel forever.
> **Joshua 4:5-7**

I did a bit of research on the practice of setting up stones and found it was common practice in the Middle East to erect stones. They did so to honor gods, declare covenants and treaties, and commemorate unexplained supernatural phenomena. As early as Genesis, Scripture relays instances of God's people setting up stones as reminders of their relationship with Him.

I love the idea of having visible reminders of the wonders God works in our lives. After all, we are a people of visible reminders. We have locks of our baby's hair, their first tooth, wedding bands, college T-shirts, sports caps, photographs, and selfies. We have all manner of paraphernalia to mark great events, meaningful allegiances, and even everyday moments.

> **If you had kept a visible reminder of each miracle God has wrought in your life, what would those reminders be?**

The entire Bible is a repetition of God's central message to us—I will save you; I love you; I want to be with you! He reminds us so often because He is aware that we are such a deeply forgetful people. Joshua knew this about God's people, and he too reiterated in action and deed that the story of the stones was to be passed down from generation to generation.

The entire Bible is a repetition of God's central message to us — I will save you; I love you; I want to be with you!

And Joshua set up at Gilgal the twelve stones they had taken out
of the Jordan. He said to the Israelites, "In the future when your
descendants ask their parents, 'What do these stones mean?' tell them,
'Israel crossed the Jordan on dry ground.' For the LORD your God
dried up the Jordan before you until you had crossed over. The LORD your
God did to the Jordan what he had done to the Red Sea when he dried
it up before us until we had crossed over. He did this so that all the
peoples of the earth might know that the hand of the LORD is
powerful and so that you might always fear the LORD your God.
Joshua 4:20-24

Earlier in this lesson, I emphasized the importance of noting that the miracle wrought by God COMPLETELY dried the Jordan riverbed. Notice too how many times a derivation of the word "dry" is used by Joshua in the passage above. I count three references. Clearly, God wanted it perfectly understood that the ground once covered by a raging river was completely dry! God did not want the Israelites or their descendants to miss out on this miracle. He wanted every believer throughout all of history to grasp the detailed level with which He attends to our lives in miraculous majesty.

Traditions and stories are powerfully connective tools that bind a family and community together. Take a moment to write down and consider what stories your family holds dear. Think about what role of prominence God has in your family's treasured stories.

5.5: Living Stones

In you our ancestors put their trust; they trusted and
you delivered them. To you they cried out and were saved;
in you they trusted and were not put to shame.
Psalm 22:4-5

This Psalm above was penned by David. How might David have come to believe that God was faithful to save?

David grew up hearing and living the stories of God's faithfulness. The tales of memorial stones must have been as familiar to him as the bedtime stories we tell our own children. Perhaps, in his travels, he even saw the stones himself.

How will your children know about God's powerful intercessory character?

It is clear God intended that the stones remind us of His faithfulness to save. The references to stones and their use as symbols of remembrance become even more personal in the New Testament when Peter uses the standing stone imagery to describe believers as "living stones."

You also, like living stones, are being built into a spiritual
house to be a holy priesthood, offering spiritual sacrifices
acceptable to God through Jesus Christ.
1 Peter 2:5

Since God meant stones to be reminders of His faithfulness to save, this infers that you and I, as living stones, can be reminders of His saving grace. Our life in Christ not only is a reminder to us, but also to all who witness what we overcome in His name.

Peter calls all believers to become living, breathing, professing stones of remembrance. List some ways you are living your faith to demonstrate the saving work of God.

In Revelation, we see another use of the stone imagery when John reports what Christ says to all the churches. We looked at this verse in an earlier lesson to relate the special relationship inherent in a name shared only between you and Jesus. Let's look at it again and marvel at the glory of God's affection for us.

> Whoever has ears, let them hear what the Spirit says to the churches. To the one who is victorious, I will give some of the hidden manna. I will also give that person a white stone with a new name written on it, known only to the one who receives it.
> **Revelation 2:17**

I can't wait to read my new name on that stone from the hand of Christ! I imagine it might be a name that reflects the special relationship we have developed over the years—a name like the endearing nicknames friends and family give each other after years of so intimately sharing their lives in all the glory and grime. Most certainly it will be a name I will greatly treasure. And the stone it is written on will be my lifetime reminder that I am saved by Christ.

Let's deepen our commitment to share our heart with God in every situation. He is faithful to restore, refresh, and reenergize us for the work He has called us to do. In the complexity of our children's needs and the temptation to sink into our own emotional turmoil, we can scream our hearts out to the Father, and He will make us living stones. What testimony could be more miraculous than parents of special needs children living visible lives of God-ordained joy!

Small Group Discussion

Study Five - You Can Let It All Out With God

After you have individually reviewed the readings and reflection questions, meet with your small group using the suggested format below:

Believe: We can share every inch of our lives with God.

Scripture Reading: What does this verse mean to you?

> Taste and see that the LORD is good;
> blessed is the one who takes refuge in him.
>
> **Psalm 34:8**

Engage: Review the questions below and allow each person to participate in the discussion.

5.1
- **(1) In what ways can you relate to the distress David exclaims in the Psalms?**
- **(2) Discuss times it has been easy and times it has been difficult for you to pour out your heart to God and think of Him as your refuge.**

5.2
- **(3) Why can God be trusted to provide the form of healing you need?**
- **(4) Share examples of how the Word of God was your "spoonful of sugar" during a difficult situation.**

5.3
- **(5) Have stories others shared with you about how God has intervened in their lives been a comfort to you? If yes, share one.**
- **(6) When has God asked you to go through an impossible situation and how did you feel about this?**

5.4
- **(7) How has God gotten you through a tough situation?**
- **(8) What has been the benefit to you of waiting on God's timing for a promise from God to be fulfilled?**
- **(9) What would your visible reminder of a miracle God worked in your life look like?**

> (10) What stories of God's saving grace have been handed down as a matter of tradition in your family?

5.5 | (11) What can you do to ensure your children come to know of God's powerful intercession?

> (12) What does it mean to you to think of yourself as a living stone of God's saving grace?

Celebrate: We can tell God everything and anything in a roar, a whisper, a sigh, a groan, and between tears. He hears us, gives us rest, heals us, and calls us into community with those who share our burdens. He provides stones of remembrance and makes of us living stones. How sweet is His Word on our tongues.

Pray: *Lord, how honored are we to bring our burdens in wails and whisperings to Your throne, for we know You incline Your ear toward us. When we faint with weariness, You give us rest; when the hurt runs too deep, You heal us. You put in our paths a community whose burdens we share and who will share ours. Thank You for giving us solid memories of Your miracles in our lives and making of us living memorial stones of Your provision, protection, and salvation. Amen.*

(Add prayer requests and specific praise reports from the group.)

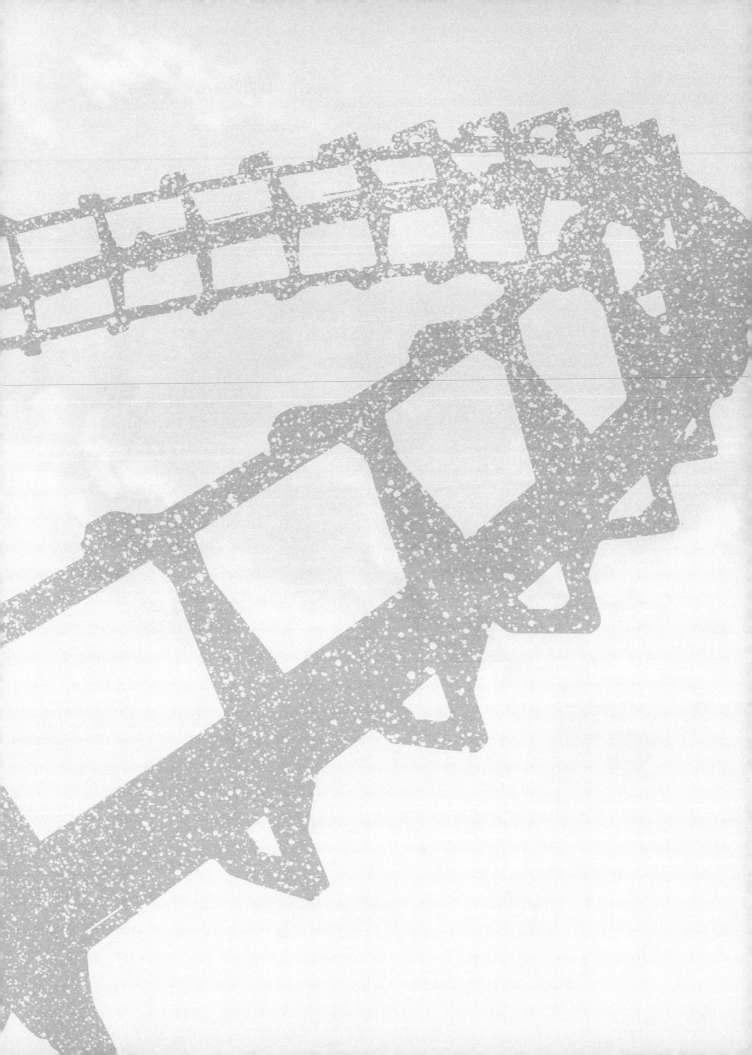

Therefore, since we are surrounded
by such a great cloud of witnesses,
let us throw off everything that hinders
and the sin that so easily entangles.
And let us run with perseverance
the race marked out for us.
Hebrews 12:1

STUDY SIX
GOD ORDAINS A GREAT CROWD OF WITNESSES

Find Camaraderie With a Train Full of Riders

We can often feel isolated in parenting our special needs children. Families feel uninvited, judged, and even shunned. Describing her family life after her son was diagnosed, a dear friend remarked, "It's as if my whole family was diagnosed with autism." A special needs diagnosis is definitely a life changer of grand proportions, and people not living the special needs life have an understandably hard time truly fathoming what parents and families experience. I had three older girls when Mia was born, and I can attest to the fact that my entire definition about what it meant to parent changed with Mia's arrival.

We need people around us who understand this—people on the outside of our individual day-to-day routines who are really on the inside because their daily journeys so closely resemble our own. Hebrews 12:1 tells us we have a great crowd of witnesses with which to surround ourselves. The stories of some of these witnesses are included in Scripture to strengthen us. In Hebrews, Paul describes what witnesses of Christ endured.

Take note of the hardships faced by those in Hebrews 11:36-38:

Some faced jeers and flogging, and even chains and imprisonment.
They were put to death by stoning; they were sawed in two; they were killed by
the sword. They went about in sheepskins and goatskins, destitute, persecuted
and mistreated—the world was not worthy of them. They wandered in
deserts and mountains, living in caves and in holes in the ground.

These people clearly faced enormous difficulties! I have learned from necessity that when I am feeling unfairly burdened, a wide-eyed look at the circumstances of those near and far to me powerfully deflates my "woe is me" pity-party. Ironically, the very fact that others experience trials can both comfort AND exhort me—misery does love company. Oddly though, company generally makes us feel less miserable. Communing with those walking in our shoes actually defeats misery. In fact, the more we let others with similar troubles into our lives, the more apt we are to start comforting them. It is actually more akin to the saying, "A joy shared is doubled; a sorrow shared is halved."

God clearly instructs us to take our troubles to Him as shown in the passages below:

Cast your cares on the Lord and he will sustain you.
Psalm 55:22

Peace I leave with you; my peace I give you. I do not give to you as the world gives.
Do not let your hearts be troubled and do not be afraid.
John 14:27

Do not be anxious about anything, but in every situation, by prayer and petition,
with thanksgiving, present your requests to God. And the peace of God, which
transcends all understanding, will guard your hearts and your minds in Christ Jesus.
Philippians 4:6-7

He also, just as clearly, calls us to bear each other's burdens. Galatians 6:2 says, "Carry each other's burdens, and in this way you will fulfill the law of Christ." Therefore, we are to make a point to actively be aware of others' burdens, be of assistance to them, and pray earnestly for them. Caring for each other in this way builds community. When we come together in our Christian community, we lay these shared burdens at the feet of Jesus, and He proves faithful, time and time again, to sustain us.

Study Six – God Ordains a Great Crowd of Witnesses

6.1: Called Into Communities of Faith

The Bible is clear that, while the acceptance of Jesus as Lord and Savior is an individual experience, the faith life of all Christians is meant to be experienced in community. And since our entire lives are designed to center on our faith, so we too should be sharing both the trials and joys of our lives in Christian community. Hebrews 10:24-25 gives us practical guidance in this regard: "And let us consider how we may spur one another on toward love and good deeds, not giving up meeting together, as some are in the habit of doing, but encouraging one another—and all the more as you see the Day approaching." The ESV translation uses the words, "stir up" in the place of "spur." The visual of stirring up and spurring one another along in good works is a powerful one.

We have the opportunity in this Bible study group to stir each other up. We are in good Christian company. Gathered together for this study are people who feel and live very similar experiences. We have come together to connect with each other. We are parents whose disparate situations have their own unique tribulations, yet we share a common response—the response of faith.

Faith is the response we need to be constantly reminded to apply. We can learn more about doing this from each other. We learn from watching how others handle situations of joy and challenge both inside and outside our community circles. Sometimes, we are inspired not to take a low road when we watch someone else travel it. Other times we are lifted onto a higher road by the way another person tackles the twists and turns. We can find genuine encouragement in each case because both lead us to a better place.

I met a woman who had recently adopted a child she had been fostering. Many foster parents are amazing people, and adoption takes the commitment to an entirely new level. I was in awe of her service to the children she had fostered and awestruck by the fact that the child she had adopted had significant special needs. Before meeting her, I used to think and say that I would not wish the trials of raising a special needs child on anyone. But after speaking with her, I began to understand that life had not "saddled" her with a special needs child, she had chosen to raise one. This inspired me to view raising Mia as a privilege and to keep choosing to acknowledge this privilege through every difficult and harrowing kerfuffle.

Faith is the response we need to be constantly reminded to apply.

Share a story about a parent and/or family whose response to some aspect of their journey particularly inspired you.

Over the past years, I have regularly attended meetings with a group of women whom I have met only because we all have children with special needs. These women have become dear friends. On more than one occasion, we have turned to one another to say, "Wow, I am so glad to be here with you, so glad that I know you! But my goodness, I hate the fact that I have to!"

As we have discussed in the previous session, it is okay to have less than loving feelings toward the difficulties of our lives. But when we are called into community with people who can help us muster the courage to overcome them, it is critical to let gratefulness wash over us with every bit of encouragement they provide us. Mia's diagnosis has led me into community with so many people I would not otherwise have met—people who comfort me and people to whom I have, in turn, been a comfort. God can, and will, take every tough thing we hand over to Him and fill it with His inexhaustible grace.

Make a list of the people who have shared your burdens and perhaps those whose burdens you have shared. Offer up a prayer of thanksgiving for both groups of people. And if it feels right to you, consider coming up with a simple way to show both groups of people how grateful you are to have walked the Christian burden-sharing journey together.

6.2: Lifted to Build Up the Community

Access to a community of faithful believers is a gift. We receive so much from regularly meeting with other Christians at church, in small group Bible studies, and one-on-one. We are taught, inspired, healed, set right, prayed for, loved and encouraged. And not only do we receive wonderful gifts from those God puts in our lives, but Scripture tells us we have each been uniquely gifted to share our talents.

And who knows but that you have come to your royal position for such a time as this? Esther 4:14

In meditating on God's purpose for my life, I often recall this verse from Esther 4:14 "And who knows but that you have come to your royal position for such a time as this?"

Have you ever wondered, when reading the story of Esther, whether she regarded her unexpected ascension to queen of all Persia as a "royal" position? Perhaps she had other dreams for her life, perhaps she envisioned a different kind of home and married life than the one she had with King Xerxes. Consider this Scripture verse from 1 Peter 2:9: "But you are a chosen people, a royal priesthood, a holy nation, God's special possession, that you may declare the praises of him who called you out of darkness into his wonderful light."

> **In light of the verses above, is it possible, despite the outward appearance of our circumstances, that when we fellowship with God, the positions we occupy are indeed "royal" positions, having been allowed by, and elevated by, our heavenly Father? Jot down thoughts about how this might apply to some of the positions you hold.**

I have struggled mightily with the question above, especially in the early days of Mia's diagnosis. Who in their right mind, I wondered, could dub "parent of an autistic child" a royal position? Surely this autism chasm that was swallowing my dreams for my child, my family, and the possibility that I would ever retire as an empty nester, could only be considered a destructive force upon my life, not an elevating one. But God sees things differently. Matthew 23:12 tells us, "Those who humble themselves will be exalted." Raising a child with autism is humbling indeed, but Psalm 3:3 tells me that the Lord is "a shield around me, my glory, the One who lifts my head high."

Such a God-take view of our situation, allows us to understand and rise to the high calling the Lord has bestowed upon us. We are called to royal positions in the raising of our special needs children. We are called to be lights to the world as we manage our positions with the regal humility of children of God. Our positions and talents can be used first and foremost to build up His body of believers. Just as Paul called the new church at Thessalonica together, we are called to "encourage one another and build each other up" (1 Thessalonians 5:11).

If you believe that spiritual gifting is purposeful, then you can believe, too, that God knows just where you will wander in life. He knows the lives you will touch. A loving Father with this knowledge would do nothing less than grant you access to powerful equipping through His Holy Spirit. With such equipping you can, despite your perceived failings and personal trials, uniquely meet specific needs in your community.

Take a moment to reflect on how God has gifted you to serve your family and community. Are there additional ways you might serve?

We all want to fit in; we want a place to belong. Being an active member of the body of Christ means you do belong. You occupy a very special place. God gives you an effective and healing role to play. And He grants you the grace to be a recipient of the effect and healing He has equipped others to provide for your benefit. Praise the Lord for having so thoughtfully orchestrated the details of the Christian life.

6.3: Gifted to Encourage

As we discussed in the reading for 6.2, most people have a real desire to be a meaningful part of a community. I have experienced this craving countless times as I have moved to new countries, states, jobs, schools, and churches. I am sure you have heard friends and family describe their longing for deeper relationships and a place to belong. God surely placed in each believer's spirit not only an inherent desire to grow in relationship with Jesus, but also to do so in the context of community.

I just love the following analogy on Christian community written in the Christian Crier by Pastor Jack Wellman.

> A friend of mine was having a bar-b-que and I intentionally moved one coal over to the side. Eventually it started to die out and cool off. This reminded me of the need for each of us to 'stir up one another to love and to good works' because if we are off to the side, by ourselves, we tend to cool off pretty quickly. For one thing, if we are living the Christian life as a solo act, who can we stir up to love and good works? Who would there be to do the same to us? When I put that dying coal back into the rest of the coals and stirred it up, it began to get hot again and glow. That is why the author of Hebrews said we should 'not neglect to meet together'... but 'encourage one another' and even more so 'as [we] see the Day drawing near,' the 'Day' meaning the day of the Lord's return."

Pastor Wellman's analogy of the burning coal brings this powerful scriptural passage from Isaiah to mind:

> "Woe to me!" I cried. "I am ruined! For I am a man of unclean lips, and I live among a people of unclean lips, and my eyes have seen the King, the LORD Almighty." Then one of the seraphim flew to me with a live coal in his hand, which he had taken with tongs from the altar. With it he touched my mouth and said, "See, this has touched your lips; your guilt is taken away and your sin atoned for." Then I heard the voice of the Lord saying, "Whom shall I send? And who will go for us?" And I said, "Here am I. Send me!"
>
> **Isaiah 6:5-8**

Isaiah responded enthusiastically to God's call to be a burning coal among his people, and God gave a very specific commission with specific words to speak to Israel. Being commissioned by God is an incredible privilege and responsibility. Many stories in the Bible describe situations in which those called by God were downright reluctant, like Jonah and Moses, or skeptical like Gideon.

Have you ever felt you had a clear call from God yet hesitated to respond? If so, think about why you hesitated and jot your thoughts below.

There have been many times I have heard God's call to behave a certain way for the upbuilding of the faith. Sometimes, I have stepped up to His call, other times I have dawdled and even failed. When I do accept His call and His Word, when I prayerfully seek His guidance, the harvest He reaps from my words and actions is humbling and extraordinary every time, even when the only result I see is the one He works in me.

Read the following verses and note how each may have applied to you either as something you received from someone in the church or something you gave to another.

Anxiety in a man's heart weighs him down,
but a good word makes him glad.
Proverbs 12:25

Note:

> A word fitly spoken is like apples of gold in a setting of silver.
> **Proverbs 25:11**

Note:

> We who are strong ought to bear with the failings of the weak and not to
> please ourselves. Each of us should please our neighbors for their good,
> to build them up. For even Christ did not please himself but, as it is written:
> "The insults of those who insult you have fallen on me."
> **Romans 15:1-3**

Note:

At times, we may feel we don't have anything to give someone experiencing a trial in our community or in our family. Yet, the verses above speak of the positive effect the gift of an encouraging word can yield. As Christians, we know there is tremendous truth and power in the words of Scripture. When believers in Thessalonica were anxious over the plight of loved ones who had died, Paul even gives them specific words of scriptural truth to comfort one another.

There is tremendous truth and power in the words of Scripture.

> For the Lord himself will come down from heaven, with a
> loud command, with the voice of the archangel and with the trumpet
> call of God, and the dead in Christ will rise first. After that, we who are
> still alive and are left will be caught up together with them in the clouds to
> meet the Lord in the air. And so we will be with the Lord forever.
> Therefore comfort one another with these words.
> **1 Thessalonians 4:16-18**

These are words that can comfort all of us. How glorious that at Jesus' second coming all believing souls will be united with a holy body and rise to meet Christ. In fact, Paul himself was so anxious to be with Jesus that he was torn between his own ministry and leaving his earthly body to join Christ. He explains this in Philippians:

For to me, to live is Christ and to die is gain. If I am
to go on living in the body, this will mean fruitful labor for me.
Yet what shall I choose? I do not know! I am torn between the two:
I desire to depart and be with Christ, which is better by far;
but it is more necessary for you that I remain in the body.

Philippians 1:21-24

I have often felt like Paul, especially in some of our darkest times, and I have found these verses particularly consoling as the parent of a special needs child. I know Jesus has called me to this earthly special needs ministry in a very intimate manner, and I count on Him to help me fulfill this ministry. It simply makes me marvel to think that one day all the troubles we face as parents and families and the difficulties of our special needs children will be no more. What great hope we have in a very real Savior who heals, redeems, reunites, and promises to bring us to our true and glorious home with Him. He is the cure for what ails our children and consequently for what ails us as their parents! Let's share His words of comfort with everyone in need.

Take a moment to write a prayer below asking God to reveal what words He would have you speak to nurture those closest to you and those in your church and local communities?

God knows your trials and He has a plan. His plan includes the gift of community.

When the daily pressures build up, when crisis arises afresh, when we feel like it is all just too much, we have a community of believers to turn to who can say, "I know, I've been there, I will pray with you, I am here for you." We all need this kind of community, particularly if we are feeling alone in our trials and are without the positive proximal support of a close and believing extended family. God knows your trials and He has a plan. His plan includes the gift of community. He has given us the Church, and we are each important, pivotal members of His Church. Embracing and encouraging one another is our Christian calling.

> For everything that was written in the past was written to teach us, so that through the endurance taught in the Scriptures and the encouragement they provide we might have hope. May the God who gives endurance and encouragement give you the same attitude of mind toward each other that Christ Jesus had, so that with one mind and one voice you may glorify the God and Father of our Lord Jesus Christ. Accept one another, then, just as Christ accepted you, in order to bring praise to God.
> **Romans 15:4-7**

Praise God for ordaining, accepting, and encouraging church families for His people!

6.4: Indispensable and Interdependent

No matter how much the term "inclusion" is bantered about, regarding our special needs children, the early years of a diagnosis feel anything but inclusive. A labeled diagnosis often feels like a wall separating us from the other "normal" families going about what seems to be "life as usual." Far removed from this "normalcy," we are warped into a new universe completely alien to us.

The world in general is not always a hospitable place, and when special needs are added to our list of oddities, we enter a world of people and situations that often leave us feeling uninvited, troublesome, dispensable, and alone. Yet, 1 Corinthians 12:22 tells us that within the body of Christ "those parts of the body that seem to be weaker are indispensable." While we try to navigate this new terrain, it is a pivotal comfort to know our heavenly Father counts each member of His family as indispensable!

First Corinthians 12 has much to say about the unique and interdependent relationship God intends His people to have with one another. Read the full passage below and consider the questions listed after each section.

> The eye cannot say to the hand, "I don't need you!"
> And the head cannot say to the feet, "I don't need you!"
> On the contrary, those parts of the body that seem to
> be weaker are indispensable, and the parts that we think
> are less honorable we treat with special honor.
> And the parts that are unpresentable are treated with

Our heavenly Father counts each member of His family as indispensable!

special modesty, while our presentable parts need no special treatment. But God has put the body together, giving greater honor to the parts that lacked it, so that there should be no division in the body, but that its parts should have equal concern for each other. If one part suffers, every part suffers with it; if one part is honored, every part rejoices with it.

1 Corinthians 12:21-26

Do you believe every member in the church benefits the body of Christ in some unique way? Explain why you do or don't feel this is so.

How might your answer to the question above relate to someone with whom you have particular differences or difficulties within your church? How might it relate to how you feel about your special needs child's role in your church?

Consider the meaning of this passage of Scripture:

Just as a body, though one, has many parts, but all its many parts form one body, so it is with Christ. For we were all baptized by one Spirit so as to form one body—whether Jews or Gentiles, slave or free—and we were all given the one Spirit to drink. Even so the body is not made up of one part but of many. Now if the foot should say, "Because I am not a hand, I do not belong to the body," it would not for that reason stop being part of the body. And if the ear should say, "Because I am not an eye, I do not belong to the body," it would not for that reason stop being part of the body. If the whole body were an eye, where would the sense of hearing be? If the whole body were an ear, where would the sense of smell be? But in fact God has placed the parts in the body, every one of them, just as he wanted them to be. If they were all one part, where would the body be? As it is, there are many parts, but one body.

1 Corinthians 12:12-20

Have you always made it a priority in your life to belong to a Christian community? Why or why not?

Corinthians has more to say about the body of Christ.

Now you are the body of Christ, and each one of you is a part of it. And God has placed in the church first of all apostles, second prophets, third teachers, then miracles, then gifts of healing, of helping, of guidance, and of different kinds of tongues. Are all apostles? Are all prophets? Are all teachers? Do all work miracles? Do all have gifts of healing? Do all speak in tongues? Do all interpret?

1 Corinthians 12: 27-30

Are the resources, characteristics, and talents you alone have enough to sustain you? Are they enough to sustain your family? Why or why not?

I have been greatly lifted by the encouragement, gifts, and testimonies of many members of the Church. As Corinthians teaches:

There are different kinds of gifts, but the same Spirit distributes them. There are different kinds of service, but the same Lord. There are different kinds of working, but in all of them and in everyone it is the same God at work. Now to each one the manifestation of the Spirit is given for the common good. To one there is given through the Spirit a message of

wisdom, to another a message of knowledge by means of the same Spirit,
to another faith by the same Spirit, to another gifts of healing by that one
Spirit, to another miraculous powers, to another prophecy,
to another distinguishing between spirits, to another speaking in different
kinds of tongues, and to still another the interpretation of tongues.
All these are the work of one and the same Spirit, and he
distributes them to each one, just as he determines.
1 Corinthians 12:4-11

Relate a time you found yourself relying on the sufficiency of God's grace vested in a member or members of His Church.

In what ways might you better open yourself up to receiving the support of your church and local community?

How do you support your church and local community with your talents and resources?

What do you think the greatest gift you have to give to your church community might be?

6.5: A Christ Community

Imagine what the life of the church might be if each Christian in every community was able to consistently claim the role God has laid out for us. Imagine how it might feel to experience the sort of community Christ designed His Church to be. First Corinthians 12 ends in verse 31 instructing us to "eagerly desire the higher gift yet I will show you the more excellent way." This excellent way, the crème de la crème of God's gifts, is detailed in 1 Corinthians 13.

You may have read and heard this passage in 1 Corinthians 13 a hundred times or more. Read it with fresh eyes today.

If I speak in the tongues of men or of angels, but do not have love, I am only a resounding gong or a clanging cymbal. If I have the gift of prophecy and can fathom all mysteries and all knowledge, and if I have a faith that can move mountains, but do not have love, I am nothing. If I give all I possess to the poor and give over my body to hardship that I may boast but do not have love, I gain nothing.

Love is patient, love is kind. It does not envy, it does not boast, it is not proud. It does not dishonor others, it is not self-seeking, it is not easily angered, it keeps no record of wrongs. Love does not delight in evil but rejoices with the truth. It always protects, always trusts, always hopes, always perseveres.

Love never fails.
1 Corinthians 13:8

Love never fails. But where there are prophecies, they will cease; where there are tongues, they will be stilled; where there is knowledge, it will pass away. For we know in part and we prophesy in part, but when completeness comes, what is in part disappears. When I was a child, I talked like a child, I thought like a child, I reasoned like a child. When I became a man, I put the ways of childhood behind me. For now we see only a reflection as in a mirror; then we shall see face to face. Now I know in part; then I shall know fully, even as I am fully known.

And now these three remain: faith, hope and love.
But the greatest of these is love."

First Corinthians 13 does a wonderful job of summing up the paradise-designed role we are each called to fill by the power of the Holy Spirit. Note below exactly which virtue we are called to according to this passage.

This passage unequivocally calls us to love. It further spends a great deal of ink explaining both what love is and what it is not. When I reread this passage, I was struck anew with the clarity God provides on exactly how we manifest the virtue of love. He is quite clear that certain acts in and of themselves do not mark us as "lovers." Rather it is how we perform the acts named, and in fact every act, that markedly separates those who embody this virtue from those who do not. God cleverly identifies for us which behaviors and emotional tendencies to dismiss when we are actively "loving" and which to embrace.

Take a moment to comb through the passage again and use the two columns below to represent the behaviors, acts of volition, or emotions, identified as those that do or do not represent love. I will get you started.

Behaviors That Demonstrate Love

Patience

Behaviors That Can Be Done Without Love

Speaking in Tongues

Now apply the characteristics or gifts you listed in the columns above to a specific part of your life and pinpoint below what you can today to be a living, breathing replica of 1 Corinthians 13.

Small Group Discussion

Study Six - God Ordains a Great Crowd of Witnesses

After you have individually reviewed the readings and reflection questions, meet with your small group using the suggested format below:

Believe: Christ calls us to be witnesses of faith to each other.

Scripture Reading: What does this verse mean to you?

> For where two or three gather in my name, there am I with them.
> **Matthew 18:20**

Engage: Review the questions below and allow each person to participate in the discussion.

6.1
- **(1) How has another parent of a special needs child inspired you?**
- **(2) Do you have people who have shared your burdens and whose burdens you have shared?**
- **(3) How have you demonstrated your gratefulness in both cases?**

6.2
- **(4) In what ways might you consider a call to be a special needs parents a royal position appointed by God?**
- **(5) How has God gifted you to serve others?**
- **(6) Are there additional ways He is calling you to serve?**

6.3
- **(7) Discuss why you have hesitated, or might be tempted to hesitate, to respond to a call from God.**
- **(8) Looking at the verses from 6.3, list some specific spiritual gifts you have received from, or given to, others.**
- **(9) How has God lifted you with encouraging words or given you such words to speak to specific people?**

(10) How does every believer in the Church benefit the body of Christ?

(11) How can you look at those with whom you have had difficulty within your church as benefits to the church?

(12) How can pride in being a self-sufficient person help or hinder you?

(11) In what ways have you relied on the sufficiency of God's grace and the power vested in the members of His church?

6.4

(12) Why is it, or should it be, a priority in your life to belong to a Christian community?

(13) How do you regularly support your Christian community with your talents and gifts?

(14) What ways can you better open yourself up to receiving support from your Christian community?

(15) What do you feel is your greatest gifting from God?

(16) What virtue does 1 Corinthians call us to and how is it defined?

6.5

(17) What might you do specifically to be a living, breathing replica of 1 Corinthians 13?

Celebrate: We have great cause for joy in God's design of His Church. He ordained His Church to support each other in our faith walk. We are called to specific church, home, and work communities and we are gifted to build these communities up as we encourage each other. We are each indispensable and interdependent. How we are to manifest godly love is specifically laid out for us.

Pray: *We lift up each family and thank God for bringing us together in community. Help us understand how we can use the gifts You have bestowed on us to strengthen Your Church. Help us to receive from others with grace. We ask God to strengthen us and empower us to manifest godly love toward one another. Amen.*

(Add specific praise or petition from the days' discussion)

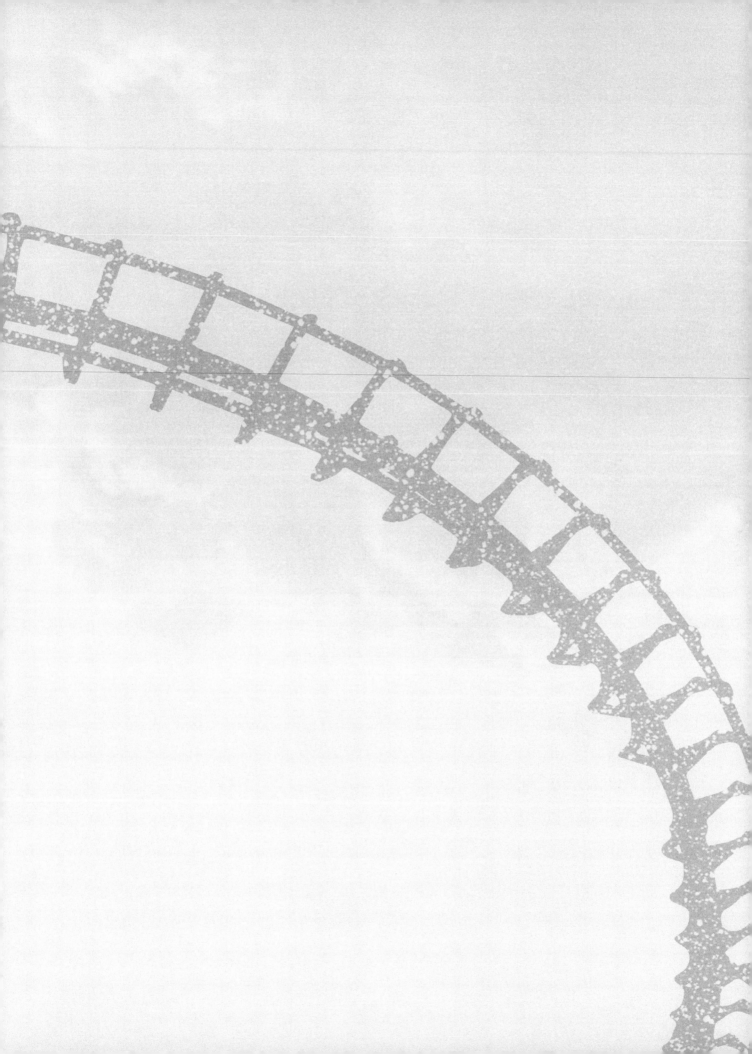

And let us run with perseverance
the race marked out for us,
fixing our eyes on Jesus,
the pioneer and perfecter of faith.
Hebrews 12:1-2

Jesus Is the One

Display Compassion for Those in the Same Seat

Jesus intends for us to grow in faith together. Maturing in our relationship with Him is a natural outgrowth of participating in our church community. Our church support groups are invaluable sources of encouragement in handling our challenges prayerfully, so it is important to understand how to successfully tap into this resource. I am a firm believer that it is our strong personal day-to-day relationships, starting with a continual partnership with God that give us the grace and wisdom to fully benefit from church support groups.

We can find no better friend, confidant, or healer than Jesus! He is the only one who saves! No matter how emotionally supportive our family or friends are, only Jesus is steady enough to handle our constant and repetitive ups and downs. He never tires of our 'same old song and dance.' He can take anything we need to dish out. He can handle anything we need to get off our chests. We can bring our worries as well as our praises to Him as many times as we need, and want, to bring them. He never tires of hearing from us.

I have found that my own emotional well-being rests very firmly on where I turn in the deeply dark predawn hours when sleep escapes me and anxiety threatens to wreak havoc with my psyche and physical health. I need a steady and wise presence in my life—someone sharing the same seat in the same roller coaster car day in, month out, year after year. For me and for all Christian believers, we are fortunate to have Jesus as our steadfast seatmate, helpmate, and champion. "For the joy set before him he endured the cross, scorning its shame, and sat down at the right hand of the throne of God. Consider him who endured such opposition from sinners, so that you will not grow weary and lose heart" (Hebrews 12:2-3).

This Scripture talks about a great joy set before Jesus that allowed Him to endure such a brutal death. What in the world could be a great enough joy to overshadow such a savage death? I crumble with gratitude to know that the joy Christ died for is my personal salvation and the salvation of every professing believer!

Christ rides the hot seat of intense trial with every person who acknowledges Him. Sometimes when things turn completely upside down for us, those we had hoped might console us keep their distance; conversely, we shut ourselves off from them. Whether we, or they, move away out of embarrassment, discomfort, callousness, or fear, the move is a painful one. Yet no such reasons of the flesh can keep God from us. He has felt the excruciating lash of mockery and desertion, and when we crash headlong into crisis, Christ rushes faster to us than we could ever rush to Him.

As I write these words, I picture Michelangelo's rendering of man and God on the Sistine Chapel ceiling. It is the perfect illustration. In the painting, the man seems to be resting lazily against the earth with one finger rather casually extended toward God. But, God is depicted with hair and garments blown back rushing toward the man with all the wind of the angels beneath Him. I love this! God cannot get to us fast enough. Imagine how fast you would run to swoop up an oblivious toddler from the path of an oncoming car. Now multiply that by godly power and you have a speed no man can fathom—this is the pace at which God reaches for us.

STUDY SEVEN – JESUS IS THE ONE

7.1: Humility

In order that we may truly experience a deep sense of satisfied purpose on this earth, God offers us His daily companionship and guidance. But in this age of copious to-do lists and prioritizing, taking advantage of God's daily presence is sometimes relegated to a small corner of our week. So, what can we do to remain connected to him? I have found Micah 6:8 to be helpful in my own quest to do just this. "And what does the LORD require of you? To act justly and to love mercy and to walk humbly with your God."

This verse highlights three elements that keep us in sync with God—acting justly, loving mercy, and walking humbly with God—an interesting combination that deserves some discussion to fully appreciate. Let's start by looking at what it means to walk humbly with God. I have discovered it is one thing to know God is always with me, yet an entirely different thing to always be with God! Let's revisit the verse we looked at from Genesis in 4.5 of Study Four. God was walking in the Garden to be with Adam and Eve, and they hid themselves. I imagine they were afraid because God had been quite forthcoming regarding the consequences of their actions and perhaps they now sensed His loving warning had been, quite literally, dead-on. Whether it was fear, pride, embarrassment, or stubborn rebellion, rather than running to God, Adam and Eve ran for cover in fig leaves and bushes. Even so, God sought them.

> Take a minute to consider what a rewrite of the Genesis story might look like if Adam and Eve had consulted God before taking devilish advice. What might it look like if they ran for Him, rather than the woods, as soon as they realized their mistake?

> When have you experienced one or both situations yourself?

Nothing in all creation is hidden from God's sight. Everything is uncovered and laid bare before the eyes of him to whom we must give account.
Hebrews 4:13

Nothing is hidden from God. Scripture attests to this truth. Hebrews 4:13 lays it out plain and simple. "Nothing in all creation is hidden from God's sight. Everything is uncovered and laid bare before the eyes of him to whom we must give account."

Still, Genesis 3:9 says, "The Lord called to the man, 'Where are you?'" Since nothing is hidden from the Lord, He clearly did not call to Adam and Eve because He did not know where they were. He knew exactly where His children were and precisely what was on their minds. Might He then have called to them to give them the choice to come to Him of their own free will? Might it be that His call of "Where are you?" was an invitation to humbly seek His help? And isn't this exactly the call He lays relentlessly and repetitively before each one of us?

Take a minute to fill in your name at the end of the question below.

And God said, "Where are you, _____?"

Now consider the possible answers in a handful of common situations you face during your day. Consider how you might seek to be more actively with God in each scenario.

Scenario   Thoughts on Being More Active With God

When God called Adam and Eve, they did come, but not with repentant hearts. Instead, they chose blame. The man blamed the woman, the woman blamed the serpent, and the endless blame-game began. The blame-game is one I have played far too many times to count, especially as a young married woman with children. The other player in the game was usually my husband, and neither of us ever won. I remember the exact day I semi-retired from the game. I say semi-retired because the Word is true and the Word says, "There is no one righteous, not even one" (Romans 3:10). So as the 'far-from-righteous' woman that I am,

I had been reading Stormie O'Martian's book, *The Power of a Praying Wife,* because I really did want to be more like the good wife Proverbs 31:10-31 lauds as "worth far more than rubies" for many reasons, including how she treats her husband—"She brings him good, not harm, all the days of her life."

To move my actions in this direction, I had been praying that the Spirit would not let me utter disrespectful things to my husband. It is the craziest thing how a prayer works even when you have completely forgotten you just prayed it. And on this day, I had forgotten and was ready to give my husband an earful, but the Spirit would not let me open my mouth. I mean it, my tongue was stilled and my lips were sealed, but those words were beating against my teeth to get out. So, I grabbed my car keys and took a long drive where my tongue was loosed so that I could scream all those words to the heavens. God took the lashing to keep my husband's spirit intact, which is exactly what Jesus did for each of us!

> **When it comes to the care of your child, have you ever felt caught in the blame-game with your spouse or other caregivers? Describe what this has been like.**

God rejects the blame-game in favor of taking our blame upon Himself—a truly astounding way to turn the tide on Satan's efforts. God's determination to be the one and only whipping post thwarted my impulse to berate my husband with a hefty dose of blame. God is faithful to His promises, and He faithfully honored my petition that the Holy Spirit check my errant impulses and grant me the humility to walk with Him. If we can believe God is the personification of goodness, and thus can be trusted to guide us well, then we are well on our way to walking humbly with Him. And in walking by His side, we gain access to behave with justice and mercy—for justice and mercy are supremely available when we let Him empower us to do His will. It is the valuing and seeking of God's opinion on every matter in our lives that allows us to act with His wisdom. We need to test our will and impulses against His faithful guidance. In doing so, we are choosing to accept His presence and walk humbly, inquisitively, and steadfastly at His side with an earnest desire to receive the power to abide by His Word with justice and mercy.

God rejects the blame-game in favor of taking our blame upon Himself.

While blame does nothing to change or better our lives just as it did nothing to reverse Adam and Eve's predicament, walking humbly with God frees us to be fully responsible for our actions.

James 1:12-14 tells us:

> Blessed is the one who perseveres under trial because,
> having stood the test, that person will receive the crown of life that the
> Lord has promised to those who love him. When tempted, no one should
> say, "God is tempting me." For God cannot be tempted by evil, nor does
> he tempt anyone; but each person is tempted when they are dragged
> away by their own evil desire and enticed.

2 Peter 1:5-8 gives further instruction:

> For this very reason, make every effort to add to your faith goodness;
> and to goodness, knowledge; and to knowledge, self-control; and to self-
> control, perseverance; and to perseverance, godliness; and to godliness,
> mutual affection; and to mutual affection, love. For if you possess these
> qualities in increasing measure, they will keep you from being ineffective
> and unproductive in your knowledge of our Lord Jesus Christ.

When we pray that God will keep us from the temptation to use blame-laced accusations to correct the perceived faults of those we love, we are in effect placing ourselves under the authority of God's judgment rather than placing others under the authority of our judgement.

To control our actions for this effect, we need to let the Spirit wield the power of the Word over all aspects of our being and our lives. This includes praying that God will let us be a vehicle for His grace upon those around us, especially those living in our own homes. When we pray that God will keep us from the temptation to use blame-laced accusations to correct the perceived faults of those we love, we are in effect placing ourselves under the authority of God's judgment rather than placing others under the authority of our judgement. I, for one, would rather God, not man, be my judge! Keeping this in mind, allows me to focus on doing "unto others, as [I] would have them do unto [me]" (see Luke 6:31). It allows me to fix my eyes on Jesus.

Have you ever had your eyes fixed on what you could do and say to save yourself or your family rather than fixing them on our one and only Savior?

Fortunately, we have a Savior who is completely able to save! But unfortunately, we often forget that we are not the Savior. We do this when we let pride and self-sufficiency get in the way of walking humbly with God. If you have not seen the movie War Room, I highly recommend its message. The movie's theme focuses on the concept of creating a strategic battle plan of prayer, rather than one of belittling, to cover the behavior of all the people in our lives and consequently to cover our behavior as well.

Start your battle plan of prayer with these familiar scriptural words from our Savior:

This, then, is how you should pray: Our Father in heaven, hallowed be your name, your kingdom come, your will be done, on earth as it is in heaven. Give us today our daily bread. And forgive us our debts, as we also have forgiven our debtors. And lead us not into temptation but deliver us from the evil one.
Matthew 6:9-13

Now take out a piece of paper and write out the details concerning the people in your life you need to cover with prayer as succinctly or as detailed as you feel led to do. Choose a Scripture verse to pray for each person. Consider placing this list somewhere you can see it each day and go to battle armed with the Word in all aspects of your life.

God's time-tested faithfulness assures us we can have confidence in His hand upon each person and circumstance in our lives, even those we feel are completely outside our control, which, as parents of special needs children, are many. Psalm 46:10 reminds us of God's command: "Be still and know that I am God." He is the God and the miracle worker we each wish we could be for our children. Humbly embrace His role and let yourself, your spouse, your family members, and your caregivers, off the hook.

Be still and know that I am God.
Psalm 46:10

Of all the options I have ever chosen to pursue in life, accepting an intimate everyday relationship with God, in which He leads the way, has been my surest blessing. However, it is also my biggest challenge. The challenge lies in letting go of my secret passages, those places I travel when I just don't want to do things God's way. You see God allows us to hide when we choose to do so because He has endowed us with free will, and God is a respecter of His gifts.

Joshua sums up the freedom God has given us to choose Him, when he speaks to the Israelites saying,

> But if serving the LORD seems undesirable to you, then choose for yourselves this day whom you will serve, whether the gods your ancestors served beyond the Euphrates, or the gods of the Amorites, in whose land you are living. But as for me and my household, we will serve the LORD.
> **Joshua 24:15**

When we choose God in every area of our lives, we accept Him as the shepherd who herds us away from danger and into green pastures. He shepherds us away from the prideful path to the one that allows us to walk humbly with Him. It is a path that supernaturally flows under our feet when we fix our eyes on Him, and it is a good path with ample room for us all!

7.2: Another Choice

Despite the choices of our ancestors, Adam and Eve, God kept reaching for them just as He keeps reaching for us. And not only does He offer Himself to us every moment of our lives, but, in His grace, He has also surrounded us with people He intends to be great blessings to us. Yet, letting people in when we feel most vulnerable, most apt to be negatively judged, requires humility.

Read the verse from Ecclesiastes and then reflect on the questions below.

> Two are better than one, because they have a good return for their labor: If either of them falls down, one can help the other up. But pity anyone who falls and has no one to help them up!
> **Ecclesiastes 4:9-10**

How easy is it for you to ask for help in raising your special needs child?

Do you operate as if you must do it all on your own?

How do you feel when people do not offer, or do not know how, to help you in the way you feel you might be best helped?

Often those we count on to offer help do so in ways that don't completely dovetail with our expectations. Just as often, we have an idea of the kind of help we want, yet we do not communicate this well. And even when we think we know what kind of help we need, God may have different plans in store for us. It is crucial to pray that God will guide us in our requests for help and give us a godly appreciation for the help He sends our way.

When the Israelites were enslaved in Egypt, God acknowledged that He had heard their cries for help, and He enlisted Moses to lead the way to freedom. In Exodus 3 verses 7 and 10 God spoke to Moses saying, "I have indeed seen the misery of my people in Egypt. I have heard them crying out because of their slave drivers, and I am concerned about their suffering … So now, go. I am sending you to Pharaoh to bring my people the Israelites out of Egypt." Though Moses had doubts about his ability to carry out this mission, he did—after a bit of haggling—accept the call. And once God's call was accepted, Moses was successful, just as God promised, in bringing the Israelites out of slavery.

Yet even after the miracle of the Red Sea crossing, the Israelites found much to complain about when things did not go as they expected. Exodus 16:2-3 says, "In the desert the whole community grumbled against Moses and Aaron. The Israelites said to them, "If only we had died by the LORD's hand in Egypt! There we sat around pots of meat and ate all the food we wanted, but you have brought us out into this desert to starve this entire assembly to death." In response to their complaints, Exodus 16:8 tells us that Moses told the people, "You will know that it was the LORD when he gives you meat to eat in the evening and all the bread you want in the morning, because he has heard your grumbling against him. Who are we? You are not grumbling against us, but against the LORD."

When reading these verses, I am struck by the thought that every time I enter into a mindset of complaint, I may actually be complaining against God. After all, God is the orchestrator of my life. So perhaps it is not my circumstances or the actions of others around me that need the most changing, perhaps it is the attitude with which I receive and perceive the help and the gifts God sends my way. End this day by asking God to open your eyes to the miracle of every bit of assistance He sends your way. Perhaps, we can even thank Him for the troubles, for surely He allows them only for our ultimate good. Ask Him to give you a heart of gratefulness.

7.3: Hold Tight

God never intended or designed us to go it alone in this world. When we acknowledge we cannot do everything ourselves, we are in effect doing exactly what our Lord is calling us to do—accepting that we need a Savior. The Savior we need is Jesus. Let Him be your daily partner, and then, with all the force of heaven and Scripture behind you, partner with your spouse as much as it is up to you to do so. God ordained marriage both for our good and His glory so hold on tight to this holy relationship.

> The man said, "This is now bone of my bones and flesh of
> my flesh; she shall be called woman,' for she was taken out of man."
> That is why a man leaves his father and mother and is
> united to his wife, and they become one flesh.
> **Genesis 2:24**

If you have a spouse, pray for a grateful heart and an appreciation for this heavenly partnership. If you are parenting without the support of a spouse, know you can count on Jesus to fill every perceived gap. He is able. Isaiah 54:5 tells us that "For your Maker is your husband—the LORD Almighty is his name—the Holy One of Israel is your Redeemer; he is called the God of all the earth."

Spouses are meant to be crucial partners as we experience life's everyday struggles and joys side by side. If it is at all within our prayer-filled abilities, it is critical to maintain a truly united bond with our spouses, particularly when troubles rock our lives. In the special needs community, the divorce rate has risen to 80 percent. How is this possible when most marriage vows include the words, "for better or for worse, for richer, or poorer, in sickness and in health, to love and to cherish from this day forward?" Isn't it strange that the very things we start our marriages pledging to stand together against are often the things that drive a wedge between us?

> The LORD God said, "It is not good for the man to be alone.
> I will make a helper suitable for him."
> **Genesis 2:18**

God tells us it is not good to be alone. He also tells us that He is always with us, so we are, in fact, never alone. We have His very real presence in our lives. And yet, above and beyond His all-sufficient presence, He is gracious to bring people into our lives that are genuine helpmates to us. Spouses are meant to be helped by, and helpers to, each other. At a time when connection with, and for, our child is what we most seek, it is crucial for parents to become a committed team.

I encourage every married person in this room to view these two transformational video studies: *Laugh Your Way to a Better Marriage* by Mark Gungor; and *Love and Respect* by Emerson Eggerich—or seek out other inspirational types of activities and seminars that will increase the joy and commitment in your marriage.

Take a moment to look up and write out these verses:

Ephesians 5:25

Ephesians 5:33

Men are called to love their wives as Christ loves the church. Women are called to show respect to their husbands. God calls us to these roles because He, being our Creator, knows what we need and how we can best participate in creating thriving, fulfilling, life-giving marriages.

> **If you are married, how might you eliminate barriers to creating a harmonious balance in your marriage, or in agreeing on how to raise your special needs child?**

> **If you are not married but are co-parenting with your child's mother or father, how can you work toward a more harmonious parenting relationship?**

> **If you are a single parent, how can you invite Christ to be a more significant partner in providing harmony in your parenting?**

On our own, we will never be 100 percent able, but we can be 100 percent God-enabled.

On our own, we will never be 100 percent able, but we can be 100 percent God-enabled. My husband and I are all too familiar with being less than sturdy in dealing with Mia's constant needs. We need God's guiding hand as we work hard to support each other, even when it seems, at times, so much more attractive to walk away. I wrote a bit of prose about our struggles equating our situation to being in the middle of a precariously swinging rope bridge over the deep ravine of our daughter's challenges.

The Bridge

You are strong when I am crumbling bone
carrying me

I rise when you are crashing timber
catching you

We stand and take each blow alternately
hurting for the other, for ourselves, our baby

You speak when my voice is swallowed
in misery's mire

I decide when your thoughts fly wild
in tornadoed tumble

We each step up to the plate, emerging from our pain,
helmeted and swinging,
seldom missing our turn at bat

But occasionally both sitting out on the same bench
weeping tears, alone in our pain, head to shoulder

We draw and lose strength knowing this crisis, this illness
can create uncrossable divides or build merciful bridges

Often, we look longingly at the divide
imagining the lightness of unleashing our burdens into its depths

Yet we remain tethered by threads of hope to the bridge
where we hold tight as it creaks and groans with the weight of us.

Christ is our hope! It is okay to feel like giving up, just know there is only one meaningful place to give it all up to—the throne room of grace. Jesus died to give us entry to this place, so it must be a pretty spectacular room. How could it be anything other, as it is the place where the Father, Son, and Holy Spirit stand ready to intervene in the most miraculous and unexpected ways.

It is okay to feel like giving up, just know there is only one meaningful place to give it all up to—the throne room of grace.

Let us then approach God's throne of grace with confidence, so that we
may receive mercy and find grace to help us in our time of need.
Hebrews 4:16

7.4: The Others

The work we do and the relationships we foster can rarely be described as "all
fun and games." There are lots of less than entertaining aspects involved. Yet, we
put ourselves out there in earthly ways for heavenly reasons. Reasons that have
nothing to do with how much we want to be involved with the situations, or even
the people, we are called to deal with each day.

Do nothing out of selfish ambition or vain conceit.
Rather, in humility value others above yourselves, not looking to your own
interests but each of you to the interests of the others.
Philippians 2:3-4

*God clearly intended
us to count on, and look
out for, each other.*

God clearly intended us to count on, and look out for, each other. So, in addition
to working hard on maintaining unity with our spouse, it is crucial to intimately
involve others in our child's life. It becomes even more crucial to bring caring
people into our life when we do not have an earthly spouse to parent alongside
us. I can tell you from years of experience, a team of caregivers who are regularly
involved in your child's life, will enrich your own, and that of your family's, in the
most unexpected ways.

Iron sharpens iron, so one person sharpens another.
Proverbs 27:17

As parents, we constantly experience the heavy weight of diagnosis—of being
told our child isn't, can't, and won't. So that we do not get buried under the
weight of buying into our child's inadequacy, it is crucial to surround ourselves
with people willing to see what our child can do and will do. It is a powerful way
to make the challenge of this diagnosis lighter! We need others sharing our ride in
a real, intimate, everyday sense.

During a particularly violent phase of Mia's development, Julie, one of Mia's therapists, shared this story with me.

"I was working with Mia at a time when she was biting constantly. Every one of the therapists and all Mia's family members had black and blue bite marks up and down their arms. I also worked for some families of typical children, and one mother asked me about my bruises, sympathetically commenting on how brave and long-suffering I must be to endure this child's behavior. But my honest response was 'Oh, no, these are my badges of honor, worn with pride, because these bites are Mia's attempts to communicate with me—to connect—coming out of her world to attach, like a pit bull, to mine!'"

If you have people like this in your life, take a moment to write a prayer of thanksgiving to God for how they help you appreciate your child and see the magic, humor, and joy of raising her/him?

If you need more of these kinds of people, write a prayer of petition asking God to bring these treasures into your life.

Ask and it will be given to you; seek and you will find; knock and the door will be opened to you. For everyone who asks receives; the one who seeks finds; and to the one who knocks, the door will be opened.
Matthew 7:7-8

God allows us to experience difficult situations and difficult people, yet He also gives us the gift of people who are delightfully easy to love. Be grateful for these people and give God unending thanks for bringing them into your life. If you desire your household to become a fountain of immeasurable blessing, surround yourself with people who champion you and your child—not in a "yes-man" way, but in an "upbuilding" way. These are the God-grounded people who will inspire and lift you, echo God's words to you when you might otherwise give up, and direct your gaze to the good, and most importantly to God, in every situation.

> Finally, brothers and sisters, whatever is true, whatever is noble, whatever is right, whatever is pure, whatever is lovely, whatever is admirable—if anything is excellent or praiseworthy—think about such things.
> **Philippians 4:8**

7.5: Possibilities for Improvement Are Limitless

Is it possible for God to heal your child? Absolutely! And we have every assurance that He will do just that for He tells us that in heaven, "There will be no more death or mourning or crying or pain, for the old order of things has passed away" (Revelation 21:4). So, we have His 100 percent guarantee that healing will come.

This promise of complete healing in an eternal paradise with Christ is a precious one and an important one. Yet, I continue to search for, long for, and pray to my God for Mia's healing every day. I know it is possible for God to richly bless and heal now. And ironically, until we reach that day of no more pain, God blesses through the very assurance that this complete healing is coming. But I have seen Him heal in the "here and now" in ways that have not necessarily involved the physical and intellectual earthly healing of my Mia. I have seen healing specifically because of the diagnosis Mia faces.

What blessings have you experienced that you might not have experienced if you were not living your unique set of circumstances and your child did not face his/her particular diagnosis?

I have learned to expect God to do great things in my life every single day, to reveal so much more than my human eyes can see. Ask Him to help you see with Spirit-directed eyes. Ephesians 3:20-21 tells us that with God all things are possible. "Now to him who is able to do immeasurably more than all we ask or imagine, according to his power that is at work within us, to him be glory in the church and in Christ Jesus throughout all generations, for ever and ever!"

I love the translation of Ephesians 3:20 in *The Message:* "God can do anything, you know —far more than you could ever imagine or guess or request in your wildest dreams! He does it not by pushing us around but by working within us, His Spirit deeply and gently within us."

God can do anything, you know —far more than you could ever imagine or guess or request in your wildest dreams!
Ephesians 3:20 (MSG)

I admire our all-knowing, all-seeing, all-present God for His dedication to the free will He gifted us. He gives us opportunities to hear and heed Him while also giving us space to turn a deaf ear to Him. We are free to walk toward or away from God deciding for ourselves which resonates more powerfully within us. I have found walking toward Him to be immeasurably more enriching than walking away. He is my daily source of strength.

> It is God who arms me with strength, and keeps my way secure.
> **Psalm 18:32**

Small Group Discussion

Study Seven - Jesus Is the One

After you have individually reviewed the readings and reflection questions, meet with your small group using the suggested format below:

Believe: Jesus saves!

Scripture Reading: What do these verses mean to you?

> It is by the name of Jesus Christ of Nazareth, whom you crucified but whom God raised from the dead, that this man stands before you healed. Jesus is "the stone you builders rejected, which has become the cornerstone." Salvation is found in no one else, for there is no other name under heaven given to mankind by which we must be saved.
>
> **Acts 4:10-12**

Engage: Review the questions below and allow each person to participate in the discussion.

4.1

(1) How does it make you feel to reflect on the idea that God is always rushing toward you?

(2) How might the world have grown up differently if Adam and Eve had run to, rather than from, God? How might this idea apply to your life?

(3) When it comes to the care of your child, have you ever been caught in the blame game?

(4) Have you ever had your eyes fixed on saving yourself or your child rather than fixing them on the Savior? How have you gone to battle through prayer?

4.2

(5) How easy is it for you to ask for help in raising your special needs child?

(6) How might it be excessively stressful to operate as if you have to raise this child entirely on your own?

(7) How do you feel when people do not offer, or do not know how, to help you in the way you feel you would best be helped?

(8) What can you do to eliminate barriers to creating a harmonious balance in your marriage, specifically as it relates to raising your special needs child?

4.3

(9) If you are not married but are co-parenting with your child's mother or father, how can you work toward a more harmonious relationship?

(10) If you are a single parent, how can you invite Christ to be a more significant partner in providing harmony in your parenting?

4.4

(11) Why is it important to have people in your life who champion your child and support your parenting?

(12) How might you bring more of these people into your life?

4.5

(13) How have you experienced blessings directly related to your child's diagnosis that you might not otherwise have known?

(14) What does the unanticipated good that often results because of a difficult situation say about God's involvement in our lives?

Celebrate: Praise God for the Holy Spirit's guidance from which we gain the ability to know when to ask for and receive help. Give thanks for the gift of Jesus' saving grace that strengthens us through relationship with Him, our spouses, and others intimately involved in our lives and the lives of our children. We are awed by the endless possibilities and power of our God.

Pray: Jesus, just to be with us, You gave everything; there is no price You did not pay. Give us the wisdom to accept Your saving grace, to ask for help when we need it, and to count as precious our spouses and all those intimately involved in our families' lives. Help us open our hearts to those You ordain to be our helpers and make us a blessing to them. Grant us the vision to recognize no task is too great and no problem too complex for us to overcome with the power of Your name. Amen.

(Pray for specific intentions of the group members.)

Open my eyes that I may see
wonderful things in your law.
Psalm 119:18

THE EYES OF THE HOLY SPIRIT OFFER A SPECTACULAR VIEW

Process the View Through God's Eyes

The view from the highest point of a roller coaster can be pretty spectacular, yet, some of us close our eyes—I did. I was one of those reluctant theme park goers dragged by friends or family onto every ride. In particular, the roller coaster ride haunted me; with the first jerk of motion, I clamped my fingers tightly around the handlebar and squeezed my eyes shut. I guess I was afraid that opening my eyes would make me even more afraid. I was essentially afraid of fear. When President Roosevelt talked about fear in his inaugural address, he defined it this way: "So, first of all, let me assert my firm belief that the only thing we have to fear is... fear itself— nameless, unreasoning, unjustified terror which paralyzes needed efforts to convert retreat into advance." My roller coaster riding technique, or lack thereof, was testimony to that truism.

Here's how I got over my roller coaster fright. A friend told us that Disney offered special "front-of-the-line" passes to special needs children, enabling the entire family to avoid the long waits for the most well-loved rides. My girls were excited. Finally, something "really good" as a result of Mia's disability! They couldn't wait to go. I talked my sisters into coming. We rented a house near the park and took all the kids to Disney. Mia didn't last long; the crowds and fast-paced rides overwhelmed her. After about an hour, my husband and I clued in to her discomfort and took her back to the rental home. We left the pass with the girls and their cousins, and they couldn't have been more pleased. Mia was a hero on that trip, because her disability landed the family that "front-of-the-line" pass!

However, before we left the park, I did agree to go on the roller coaster, and for the first time in my life, I opened my eyes on the ride. In dealing with autism and epilepsy, the concept of fear had taken on a completely different dimension for me, and the roller coaster no longer qualified on my list of things to fear. With eyes wide open, I experienced every twist, turn, and dive. I was amazed. The sun shone on the entire park and beyond. People dotted the ground like bright patches of moving color. We climbed high and plunged deep. The speed was exhilarating. It was fun and, interestingly enough, it wasn't the ride that had changed after all these roller coaster-shy years, it was my point of view. In truth, the only thing we have to fear is being outside of a committed relationship with God. When we are in right relationship, we are free to keep our eyes open in anticipation of what God will do in our lives. In Study Eight we will delve into Scripture with the aim of aligning our perspectives with the Father's.

Study Eight – The Eyes of the Holy Spirit Offer a Spectacular View

8.1: Open My Eyes Lord

Next to raising a child with autism, the fear of riding a roller coaster is dwarfed. When I opened my eyes for the very first time on the roller coaster, I felt a bit like Elisha's servant. Remember when Elisha was surrounded by the Syrian army confronting him for aiding the King of Israel? Elisha's servant woke to the sight of this great army and was sorely afraid. 2 Kings 6:17 says Elisha prayed that God would open the eyes of his servant so that he could see the vast legions of angels who stood ready to defend God's prophet, "And Elisha prayed 'Open his eyes, LORD, so that he may see.' Then the LORD opened the servant's eyes, and he looked and saw the hills full of horses and chariots of fire all around Elisha."

When I take my focus off God, autism can look like the Syrian army must have looked to Elisha's servant—relentless and impossible. I continually pray God will open my eyes, change my point of view, and let the autism army be minimized by the goodness and purpose God has planned for my child and my family. Scripture offers us a host of examples that I have found useful in refocusing my vision.

Consider where Stephen's eyes were focused in Acts 7 despite the deadly anger of a hostile mob who considered him a heretic. Refresh your memory with these words from Acts 7:55-56:

> Stephen, full of the Holy Spirit, looked up to heaven and saw the glory of God, and Jesus standing at the right hand of God. "Look," he said, "I see heaven open and the Son of Man standing at the right hand of God."

Then, we are told the crowd rushed at him, dragged him out of town, and began to stone him. This is what Stephen did while they stoned him. "Stephen prayed, 'Lord Jesus, receive my spirit.' Then he fell on his knees and cried out, 'Lord, do not hold this sin against them.' When he had said this, he fell asleep" (Acts 7:59-60). What a supernatural connection to the Lord this man experienced! He chose to see the mercy and glory of the Lord rather than the hate and cruelty of those stoning him. Scripture reveals this story to let us know we too can experience this supernatural connection.

Often opening our eyes to God, quite literally, means closing them to what the world wants us to see. Christ blinded Saul on the road to Damascus as he

141

journeyed to arrest Christ's followers. He did so to show Saul just how blind he actually was. After Saul's encounter with Christ, Scripture tells us Ananias laid hands on Saul and "immediately, something like scales fell from Saul's eyes, and he could see again" (Acts 9:18). The scales of errant vision fell from his eyes and Saul's sight was made whole in the truth of Christ.

> **Have you experienced any blindness caused by the scales of errant vision? Is there any situation or person you are having trouble seeing with "Christ-clear" eyes?**

Perhaps you have prayed over a certain situation but still feel you could be looking at it with more enlightened eyes. When Jesus healed the blind man in Bethsaida, Scripture says, "He took the blind man by the hand and led him outside the village. When he had spit on the man's eyes and put his hands on him, Jesus asked, "Do you see anything?" He looked up and said, "I see people; they look like trees walking around." Once more Jesus put his hands on the man's eyes. Then his eyes were opened, his sight was restored, and he saw everything clearly" (Mark 8:23-25).

We need Christ to lay His hands on us again and again and again so that we continually progress from seeing dimly to seeing clearly. After all, can we truly appreciate what the gift of sight offers without God's perspective? Can we see truth without spiritual eyes? Don't we all need the touch of Christ to see clearly? He is the way, the truth, and the light. We cannot see when we are in darkness. We need light to see. And the only light that moves us on our way toward 20/20 vision is the true light of Christ.

Even as professing believers, improving our spiritual vision is a constant process. Often our individual blind spots prevent us from accurately perceiving people and situations. The blinders that get in our way can include worry, lack of trust, a sense of entitlement, insecurities, or preconceived notions that stubbornly serve no one. Without God's Word and the interpretation of the Holy Spirit, we can become trapped in a "not-so-fun" house of mirrors where nothing appears as it actually is and everything is seen out of proportion.

Take a moment to write a prayer to God. Ask Him to reveal to you every scale or blinder on your eyes. Ask Him to remove anything keeping you from the truth God wants you to see. Pray He will open your eyes to see clearly.

With all the craziness, and often otherworldliness, of the situations which special needs families face, we need to find inspired, spiritual ways to look at our circumstances. Mia's needs are pressing on many fronts for my family, not the least of which is financial. I remember one particularly lean time when even grocery money had run out. It was a rainy day, and I sat at home watching the rain pour copiously down outside as I wept sorrowfully inside. I prayed for peace and provision for my family, and I prayed for the weeping world. Then quite suddenly, a full and bright rainbow appeared outside my window. With camera in hand, I rushed out into what was now a "sun-shower." I was completely convinced, in the full power of Scripture, that this bow in the sky was God's very great assurance.

Tears and joy, rain and rainbow, I snapped photo after photo. As I was doing so, a neighbor pulled up and stopped her car motioning me to come over. "What are you doing out in the rain?" she asked. I pointed her gaze in the direction of the rainbow. She suggested we admire it together and told me to hop in the car. I hesitated, but she was sweetly persistent, and when I did climb in her van, she naturally asked me how things were going. We had been in a Bible study together so she knew about some of our struggles with Mia and finances. As we talked, I started sobbing and she started beaming. "Elizabeth! Look!" she said as she pulled out quite a bit of money. "I never carry cash, and even as I got this money out of the ATM today, I didn't know why I was doing it. Now I do. God meant this for you."

Of course, I told her I could not accept the money. But she was quite certain of God's will. And as we talked, I began to see God had both rainbow and pot of gold planned for me that day. It was incredibly humbling and uplifting. Who but God can match those two emotions with such miraculous precision?

My choices were outlined clearly for me that day. I could zero in on the dark cloud, or I could petition the Lord to open my eyes to the rain-delivered rainbow. God always does exceedingly more than we expect. And He once again reminded this forgetful woman that He is faithful to His Word. With grace undeserved, He delivered His assurance through a bow of glorious color and a stack of twenty dollar bills, each bill printed with familiar words that now took on an infinitely more personal and renewed meaning—"In God We Trust!"

8.2: Lighting Up Every View With Godly Vision

Cultivating a healthy world and life view is no small feat. There are so many pulls to look cross-eyed at a world gone terribly wrong, to view every situational glass as half empty rather than half full. Luckily, Christians have access to the corrective lens of Christ. Both Matthew and Luke record Christ's wisdom regarding the eye as the light and health of the body.

> The eye is the lamp of the body. If your eyes are healthy,
> your whole body will be full of light.
> **Matthew 6:22**

Luke records these same words in chapter 11 verses 33 and 34 and elaborates further in verse 36:

> Therefore, if your whole body is full of light, and no part of it dark,
> it will be just as full of light as when a lamp shines its light on you.
> **Luke 11:36**

> **How would you rate the health of your eyes in terms of what
> filters you have in place to make sense of the sights you see?
> Consider whether these filters are of a godly or worldly origin
> and consequently how well they serve you.**

To clarify my perspective, writing has always been one of the ways I attempt to make useful sense of my frustration, urgency, and despair. God has been faithful in directing my pen to reframe some of life's most trying experiences. Mia's developmental dance is one area in which I am constantly in need of perspective shifts. She has a very unusual developmental progression. She makes leaps in ability very unexpectedly and then takes weeks, even months, or years to repeat the performance. Her speech, in particular, has taken painfully long to progress following a "one step forward then totally gone" pattern. Mia was six years old before she uttered a sentence any outsider could understand. I wrote the following piece about my deep desire to hear Mia speak.

Where Do They Go

I stood at the opened refrigerator door contemplating breakfast
when I heard your small voice enunciate with shocking clarity,
"I want juice."

Startled by this first, a full sentence of three remarkably crafted words,
I hurried to honor your fortuitous request
while applauding you with enthusiastic praise,
"Nice asking! I love to hear your words!"

Later that same day I offered you more juice
hungry to hear those orchestral notes once more.
But you could not reach them
and despite your excitement to consume my offering
you managed only a slurred resemblance to "juice."

Where do they go, those perfectly formed intonations,
what black hole swallows them leaving your tongue thick and clumsy?
Yours is a pattern of speech that ebbs and flows
as if you have installed a regulatory dam
controlled by some fickle gatekeeper.

Or perhaps there is more purpose in your auditory dance,
quickening and falling mute to more fully seduce my greedy ears,
ensuring you will always have a captive audience
listening through the silence with rapt attention
for the next symphonic movement.

Writing the piece "Where Do They Go" took me from looking at Mia's verbal dance with a very heartbreaking perspective to one of humor, gratefulness, and hopeful expectation. It helped me look past the difficult parts with a nod of "Okay, I know you are there," to find the really life-changing parts—the parts I may have never had the opportunity to know in other circumstances, and certainly can't see if I don't ask God to remove the scales from my eyes.
The situations we face with our children are no walk in the park. They are real, raw, and ravaging. The only way to get beyond the worldly view of "impossible situation" is to focus our eyes on the only one for whom nothing is impossible—Our God and Savior.

> Lift up your eyes and look to the heavens: Who created all these?
> He who brings out the starry host one by one and calls forth each
> of them by name. Because of his great power and
> mighty strength, not one of them is missing.
> **Isaiah 40:26**

Describe a time you were looking at a situation one way and God opened your eyes to look at it another way?

Is there a viewpoint you are holding right now that is not serving you or your family well? If so, ask God, whose power is great enough to keep every starry host in its place, to show you what He sees. Ask Him to give you God-colored glasses that paint the world from the palette of His perspective.

8.3: Obstacles or Opportunities

In moments of self-doubt, I find myself asking God what He sees in me and why, in heaven's name, He sticks with me. Scripture tells me He sees all. He knows my desires, disappointments, dreads, fiascos, failures, and fears. He sees my villainous moments and my heroic ones. He sees me hunched over in heartbreak, shattered in shock, vexed by vengeance, irrationally irate, fuming over unfair treatment, and devastated over disaster. He often sees me searching for answers in all the wrong places, but He also sees me touched by the Spirit. In those moments, I experience colossal compassion, divine delight, lavish love, and selfless sacrifice. Through it all, He adores me because His vision of my character is filtered through His unimaginable love.

When I contemplate His view of me, I am called to examine the way I view others. Do I see their real concerns—the ups and downs that line that track of their lives—their hurts, hardships, and victories? Do I see them in a way that makes me yearn to help them, build them up, empathize and fellowship with them? Or do I focus my vision on how they inconvenience me, annoy me, misunderstand me, or detract from my happiness or worldly gain?

For example, when I consider how Mia's needs necessitated the hiring of therapists, my initial reaction is "this rots!" It is an awful lot of work finding, training, and paying people to be with my child! Yet, over a 15-year time span, I have employed more than 50 people to work with Mia, and the insights about her character, the loving contributions to my family, and the lasting friendships created are gifts I have no words to measure!

As I strive for a life of more grace-filled action, I often imagine how I might behave differently if I had a mirror in front of my face in the car, at the store, at the license bureau, the doctor's office. Or better yet, I imagine there is a video camera transmitting all I do on a reality TV show called "Christian Lives." The thought of exposing my Christian walk to that kind of public view makes me shutter. Even one "unchristian" moment can overshadow a hundred random acts of kindness. What kind of Christian example would I portray?

> **When you look at people and the circumstances they create in your life, do you see obstacles or opportunities?**

Read these verses detailing how Jesus viewed others and circle the common word.

When he saw the crowds, he had compassion on them, because they
were harassed and helpless, like sheep without a shepherd.
Matthew 9:36

When Jesus landed and saw a large crowd,
he had compassion on them and healed their sick.
Matthew 14:14

Jesus called his disciples to him and said, "have compassion for
these people; they have already been with me three days
and have nothing to eat. I do not want to send them away
hungry, or they may collapse on the way."
Matthew 15:32

Jesus had compassion on them and touched their eyes.
Immediately they received their sight and followed him.
Matthew 20:34

Filled with compassion, Jesus reached out his hand and
touched the man. "I am willing," he said. "Be clean!"
Mark 1:41

When Jesus landed and saw a large crowd, he had compassion
on them, because they were like sheep without a shepherd.
So he began teaching them many things.
Mark 6:34

How would those witnessing your actions describe the sentiments you have for others? Fill in the blanks below with your name and a descriptive word that describes how you typically view others.

_____(your name) was filled with _____(an emotion) when he/she gazed upon the crowds.

Now think about the Christian example you want to be for others and fill out the sentence with how you would like it to read.

_____(your name) was filled with _____(an emotion) when he/she gazed upon the crowds.

Christ is our very real role model. He looked at others with compassion. And He further instructs us, "See that you do not despise one of these little ones. For I tell you that their angels in heaven always see the face of my Father in heaven" (Matthew 18:10). Ask the Holy Spirit to empower you with godly sight that you may never look down upon, or despise, any of God's little ones for we are all His little ones!

> *Christ is our very real role model. He looked at others with compassion.*

8.4: If All I Have Is a Hammer

As we work to cultivate a point of view that builds a positive attitude, we are also responsible for helping others see their way to a positive attitude, especially as it relates to our special needs child. The problem for many of us is that we have grown accustomed to fighting for every inch in the world of education and social acceptability for our child. In this battle, we often get used to wielding the wrong kind of hammer in our efforts to pound out the results we desire.

You know the saying, "If all you have is a hammer, everything looks like a nail." Sometimes, we can be so angry, so used to disappointment and rejection that we are ready to strike at anything that remotely resembles a difficulty for us, even with people who are trying to help us.

> **Have you been wielding a hardship hammer? If so how has this manifested?**

There is another way to use the hammer of hardship. Do you remember the song by Peter, Paul, and Mary called "If I Had a Hammer"? The songwriter says that if he had a hammer, he would use it throughout the day and all over the countryside. He would use it to extinguish danger and create love between people. Such lyrics certainly describe an entirely novel use for a hammer. A hammer bent on pounding out love makes a soothing noise. My prayer for all parents of special needs children is that we may come to wield our hammer of hardship with such grace! In doing so, we can become the kind of role models this world so sorely needs. Let me tell you how I discovered the value of this very thing through trial and error.

A hammer bent on pounding out love makes a soothing noise.

After being ousted from a neighborhood playgroup because of Mia's behaviors and a few mothers' fears that Mia's autism might somehow contaminate their children, I had quite a bit of trepidation about ever attempting to join another neighborhood activity. After many years and by the grace of God, I mustered up the courage to put Mia on the community swim team. I wrote a letter to all 80 swim families detailing Mia's strengths and weaknesses and how our family intended to assist her in the swim team effort and in what areas she would need support from the team. I asked the coordinator of the program to send this letter out for me.

Well, the response I got was truly astounding! I received emails, and was approached at swim meets by parents, thanking me for being both brave and generous enough with my time to explain Mia's behaviors and needs to them. These people and their children rose magnanimously to the expectation of compassion that our letter had invited them to experience. They began to view my socially awkward and unpredictably impulsive Mia in an entirely new light. That summer, Mia was the most cheered for swimmer on the team, even though she never finished a single race.

> Think about how you might turn a hammer of hardship into a hammer of grace in a situation you are currently facing.

Let's commit together to lift our eyes to the Father in all circumstances, and thereby, be an inspiration to others and, consequently, a lifter of our very own souls.

> I lift up my eyes to the mountains—
> where does my help come from?
> My help comes from the LORD,
> the Maker of heaven and earth.
> He will not let your foot slip—
> he who watches over you will not slumber;
> indeed, he who watches over Israel
> will neither slumber nor sleep.
> The LORD watches over you—
> the LORD is your shade at your right hand;
> the sun will not harm you by day,
> nor the moon by night.
> The LORD will keep you from all harm—
> he will watch over your life;
> the LORD will watch over your coming and going
> both now and forevermore.
> **Psalm 121:1-8**

8.5: Give What We Want to Receive

You may all be familiar with the infamous sojourn out in public that so many of us will face or have faced with our child. The "poor pitiful child," "poor parent," or even "you are a bad parent with an unruly child" looks which we feel burning into us, or that we may even inflict on ourselves. In the world of autism, I have heard tales of a woman who dressed her child in a T-shirt reading, "I have autism. What is your problem?" and another who made up cards to pass out to onlookers saying, "I am doing the best I can; my child has autism," and describing a bit about autism.

I too needed a new response to replace the tearful, gut-wrenching reactions I erupted into upon each grocery store visit. That new response was mapped out for me on one "never routine" day of grocery shopping with my socially inappropriate Mia. It was a turning point for me and I wrote about it in a piece called "Swat."

Swat

In the grocery store, I set you down momentarily
to pull a stubborn cart from its nested bunch.

You run straight into a pair of bare legs
and begin assaulting stationary thighs with baby slaps and painful pinches.

An irate face jerks down, eyes glaring with intolerance,
annoyed hands swatting the air surrounding you
as if you were a more than pesky fly.

I snatch you up both horrified at your actions
and astounded by your victim's response.

I place you in the seat of our freed carriage
and pause to consider confronting this battered woman,
defensively explaining your lack of control
and indignantly demanding an explanation for her own.

But I pass on, suddenly believing the lesson was for me,
for how could I ask her to release her shortsighted,
incriminating judgment of you and find compassion,
when I still stood, paradoxically, in reproachful judgment of her.

Be the first to withhold judgment.

That trip to the store was a pivotal experience that helped me turn self-pity into an opportunity to offer the compassion I so desperately wanted from others. It taught me to be the first to withhold judgment. It taught me that I needed to be the first to give what I wanted to receive.

Relate a story about a difficult outing you experienced with your child. How did you turn, or could you have turned, this into an opportunity to show and inspire compassion?

Scripture instructs us,

> Do not judge, or you too will be judged. For in the same way you judge
> others, you will be judged, and with the measure you use, it will be
> measured to you. "Why do you look at the speck of sawdust in your
> brother's eye and pay no attention to the plank in your own eye?
> How can you say to your brother, 'Let me take the speck out of your eye,'
> when all the time there is a plank in your own eye? You hypocrite,
> first take the plank out of your own eye, and then you will see clearly
> to remove the speck from your brother's eye.
> **Matthew 7:1-5**

To see through the eyes of God is to see humanity as Christ sees humanity, with unconditional love — love that sacrifices everything for the Holy Spirit-driven object of its affection.

Most Christians do not want to be hypocrites. We want the logs out of our own eyes. We want to give the things we hope to receive.

> The LORD does not look at the things people look at. People look
> at the outward appearance, but the LORD looks at the heart.
> **1 Samuel 16:7**

To see through the eyes of God is to see humanity as Christ sees humanity, with unconditional love—love that sacrifices everything for the Holy Spirit-driven object of its affection. Christ's Holy Spirit-driven object of affection is you and me. He sacrificed everything—to the point of death—to offer us intimate communion with Him. And being created in God's image, we too are destined to love sacrificially. The call to love is in every fiber of our being. We can choose what, who, and how to love, but we cannot choose whether to love.

We need someone daily directing our gaze to Christ. Jesus gave us this person in the form of the Holy Spirit.

As believers, we are fortunate that the Holy Spirit guides us, but we can be slow on the uptake and we can choose not to heed the guidance. The love choices we make directly impact the quality and outcome of our lives and of the lives of those around us. Sadly, the objects of our human affection can often lead us down very dangerous roads. To have our sight corrected, enhanced and restored by Christ, we must choose to know Him and His teachings. We need to let the Holy Spirit work in us, revealing God's Word afresh and enabling us to keep His Word active and alive in our daily walk.

The next day John saw Jesus coming toward him and said,
"Look, the Lamb of God, who takes away the sin of the world!
John 1:29

John the Baptist was the first person to publicly point the eyes of God's people to Jesus Christ as Savior. Even today, we need someone daily directing our gaze to Christ. Jesus gave us this person in the form of the Holy Spirit. Allowing our focus to be Christ-targeted through the Holy Spirit is so key, because when we fix our eyes on Jesus, we land a seat with the best view on the roller coaster. It is Christ's promise of an eternal resurrected life free from pain that keeps my HOPE alive! Seeking and finding God everywhere, all the time, is our strength and our inheritance.

Look to the LORD and his strength; seek his face always.
Psalm 105:4

The Lord's strength is a gift He longs to give us.

Read the Scripture below, then personalize it by rewriting it at the bottom of this page and inserting the word 'my' for 'your' and 'I' or 'me' for 'you.'

I pray that the eyes of your heart may be enlightened in order
that you may know the hope to which he has called you, the
riches of his glorious inheritance in his holy people.
Ephesians 1:18

Small Group Discussion

Study Eight - The Eyes of the Holy Spirit Offer a Spectacular View

After you have individually reviewed the readings and reflection questions, meet with your small group using the suggested format below:

Believe: The eyes of the Spirit will show us godly visions.

Scripture Reading: What does this verse mean to you?

> Look, he is coming with the clouds, and every eye
> will see him, even those who pierced him.
> **Revelation 1:7**

Engage: Review the questions below and allow each person to participate in the discussion.

8.1
- (1) When have you felt afraid of becoming more afraid?

- (2) Relate a story about how you overcame something you were formerly afraid of experiencing.

- (3) When have you encountered situations or people you have had trouble seeing with "Christ clear" eyes? How have you dealt, or are you dealing, with this issue?

8.2
- (4) How would you rate the spiritual health of your eyes?

- (5) How has God opened your eyes to see a situation differently than you had previously viewed it?

- (6) Is there any point of view you now hold on which you need God's perspective? How can you turn this over to Him?

8.3
- (7) When you look at people and the circumstances they create in your life, do you see obstacles or opportunities?

- (8) How did Jesus view others in the Scriptures discussed in 8.3?

(9) Discuss how you filled in the blanks at the end of 8.3 regarding how you look at the crowds.

8.4

(10) What does it mean to wield a hammer of hardship and how might this affect your attitudes and actions?

(12) How might you turn the hammer of hardship into a hammer of grace?

8.5

(13) How can you turn a difficult outing you have previously experienced into an opportunity to be compassionate next time you encounter those same circumstances?

Celebrate: We rejoice in allowing our eyes to be opened by the Holy Spirit living inside us. He offers us godly vision which allows us to use our crisis for good. We can view our circumstances in the light of Christ and let Him shape how we view others as we give what we want to receive.

Pray: *Lord, we long to see clearly, to have the lamp of our bodies lit by Your light. Open our eyes to what You would have us see. Give us healthy vision so that we may look with godly perspective upon our own challenges and upon others. Give us Your compassion for others. Let us be the first to give the good we wish to receive. Amen.*

(Add any individual petitions or praise reports.)

As the Father has loved me, so have I loved you.
Now remain in my love. If you keep my commands,
you will remain in my love, just as I have kept
my Father's commands and remain in His love.
I have told you this so that my joy may be in you
and that your joy may be complete.
John 15:9-11

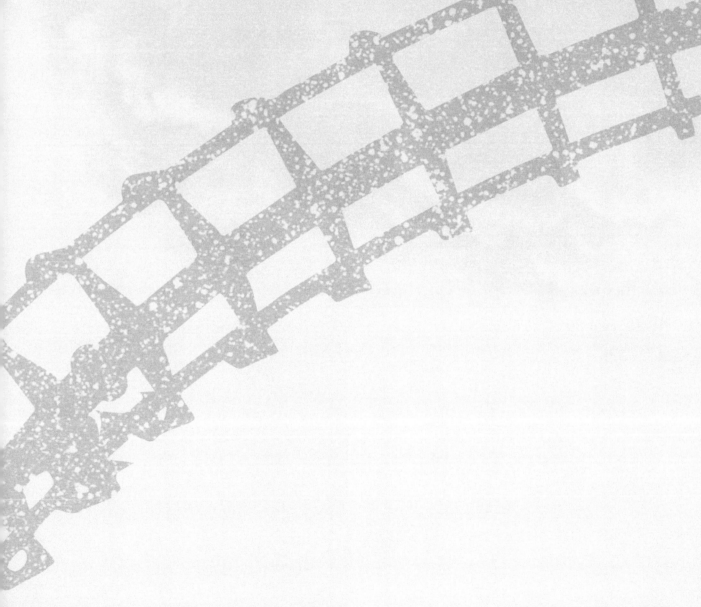

IN CHRIST WE CAN KNOW COMPLETE JOY

Let Go of the Handlebars

What an amazing gift, our dear Jesus wishes to give us all—a life of complete joy! Over my many decades, I have spent much time contemplating joy. It is something I remember praying for all my life, especially in my young adult years. When I first let go of the roller coaster handlebars after years of being afraid, I experienced joy right alongside hair-raising thrill. It was an odd comingling of emotion and left me to ponder the complete joy offered to us in Christ Jesus. I had spent many years praying for a joyful life, always assuming complete joy necessarily meant the absence of suffering. Mia's arrival on the scene challenged this assumption in a mighty way.

When Mia was first diagnosed in the hospital, I could not imagine ever experiencing joy again. So entirely consuming was my grief that no millimeter of space remained for any other emotion. I found myself no longer praying for joy, but rather, praying for an understanding of how God, and anyone on that hospital floor, could possibly feel joy when such heartbreak existed in the world. In my search for an answer, I was prompted to explore the dictionary definition of joy.

Webster defines joy as:

    1. a: The emotion evoked by well-being, success, or good fortune or
       by the prospect of possessing what one desires: delight.
      b: The expression or exhibition of such emotion: gaiety.
    2. a state of happiness or felicity: bliss.
    3. a source or cause of delight.

Other synonyms for joy are listed as: "elation, comfort, glee, humor, pride, satisfaction, wonder, cheer, ecstasy, jubilance, gladness, hilarity, merriment, mirth."

Jesus' words from John 15 offer an entirely different definition of joy. He says, "If you keep my commands, you will remain in my love, just as I have kept my Father's commands and remain in his love. I have told you this so that my joy may be in you and that your joy may be complete." Jesus is telling us joy is found through an awareness and acceptance of God's love. I don't know about you, but I desperately want to remain in God's love. Even so, as I admitted in 3.4 of Study Three, I have wondered how God could love me when I am so riddled with shortcomings. Yet, Jesus tells us we remain in God's love when we keep His commands.

In Matthew 22:37-40, He sums up those commands like this:

> "Love the Lord your God with all your heart and with all your soul and with all your mind.
> This is the first and greatest commandment. And the second is like it: Love your neighbor
> as yourself. All the Law and the Prophets hang on these two commandments."

So, it would seem He is telling us we will know complete joy when we walk in complete godly love.

I know no better way to cultivate a spirit in harmony with godly love, than to let God write His Word on my heart through the study of Scripture and the leading of the Holy Spirit. As we work through the material in Study Nine, we will look closely at Holy Scripture with the goal of fine-tuning our definition of joy to match the experience God intends for us. I pray the Holy Spirit will prepare our hearts to receive His interpretation of a joy-filled life.

Study Nine - In Christ We Can Know Complete Joy

9.1: The Source of Joy

Christopher Hitchens, an outspoken antitheist and the author of *God Is Not Great: How Religion Poisons Everything,* said in that book, "To 'choose' dogma and faith over doubt and experiment is to throw out the ripening vintage and to reach greedily for the Kool-Aid." This statement equates doubt to a well-ripened wine, while portraying faith as a sugary child's drink. This suggests that when we choose faith over doubt, we trade something of great value for something of sweet appeal, but little value. This has not been my actuality. While my relationship with God is peppered with questions, many which have yet to be answered, I have not found doubt to be a desirable vintage.

When I sank to my lowest point of despair during Mia's illness, I doubted. I doubted what Scripture taught and I even doubted my own personal experience with God. I fixated only on the heart-twisting experience of suffering over my darling daughter's illness. While I dwelt in this place of doubt, I turned away from my relationship with God in favor of dwelling on my pain. I felt certain I would never feel joy again, and I pined for past moments of joy that had now become larger than life to me.

To soothe my aching heart, I turned to the deceptively appealing pretenders of despair, blame, and anger that, like wolves in lambs clothing, stood first in line as replacements for my faith. Oddly, giving in to these tempters seemed like a great way to get some satisfying vindication. Yet these imposters did not quench my thirst, nor did they lift me to any giddy buzz. Rather they left me spiraling downward in an empty, unhappy cycle of "why me; why us?"

Praise God for faith! Doubt and painful experience imprisoned me in a pit of despair while the gift of faith filled me with the heavenly high of hope and peace. Faith proved to be my true fine wine.

We all know the story of Jesus' first miracle when He turned water into wine at the wedding in Cana. When the master of the banquet tasted the water that Jesus had turned into wine, John 2:9-10 tells us he was perplexed:

Then he called the bridegroom aside and said, "Everyone brings out the
choice wine first and then the cheaper wine after the guests have had too
much to drink; but you have saved the best till now."

In the whirl of thought that consumed me during that first hospital visit, Jesus
seemed to operate with me in just this same way—He let me taste the lesser
thirst quenchers, but stood ready to change those bitter drinks into the good stuff
of His love and salvation. John 2:11 says, "What Jesus did here in Cana of Galilee
was the first of the signs through which he revealed his glory; and his disciples
believed in him." I found my way back to believing in Him too, and how glad I am
that He opened my heart to do so.

Later in John, we read about Jesus working another kind of miracle around water
when He speaks to the woman at the well in Samaria. Jesus tells her He has a
special kind of drink for her. In John 4:13-14, He compares His offering to the well
water she came to draw:

> Everyone who drinks this water will be thirsty again, but whoever drinks
> the water I give them will never thirst. Indeed, the water I give them will
> become in them a spring of water welling up to eternal life.

When I began to sip again at the well-spring of Christ's eternal flow, I found
the determination to find my way back to joy. This set me on a thorough quest
to understand what the capability to feel joy was all about. As a first step, I
contemplated the moments I had equated with joy throughout my life.

**Take a minute to reflect on what your current definition of joy
might be. Note the circumstances surrounding times you felt
great joy.**

My recollections of joy included tender moments with family and friends, the crazy antics of children, awe-inspiring views of nature, creating a piece of art, writing, the warm supernatural peace of the Lord, and the unexpected surprises and kindnesses done for me and by me, for both scenarios bring joy. Countless memories, large and small, flooded my battle-worn heart. Reliving these snippets of bliss was assurance of joy's existence—even in the face of crisis.

God's love is our source of joy, God's nearness is our cause for rejoicing.

Armed with the certainty of joy's existence, my search of the worldly and spiritual definitions of joy helped me find my way back to experiencing it. Both offered much food for thought. Not surprisingly, however, the biblical definition was the rich source I needed to replenish my fountain of joy.

Reread John 15:9-11 on the introductory page of Study Nine or in your Bible, and then read Philippians 4:4-7 below. Consider how these two verses pinpoint the source of joy.

Rejoice in the Lord always. I will say it again: Rejoice!
Let your gentleness be evident to all. The Lord is near.
Do not be anxious about anything, but in every situation,
by prayer and petition, with thanksgiving, present your
requests to God. And the peace of God, which
transcends all understanding, will guard your hearts
and your minds in Christ Jesus.

What stands out to you in both verses as the source and reason for our joy?

Did you notice how John tells us remaining in God's love is our source of joy, and Philippians tells us God's nearness is our cause for rejoicing? These two verses and so many others identify an awareness of the loving presence of God as the source of transcendent joy. Philippians 4 further suggests in verses 8-9 that confidence in the Lord's presence leads to the release of anxiety and the freedom to experience gentleness, peace, and the contemplation of every good and true thing.

Jesus tells us He is "the way, and the truth, and the life. No one comes to the Father except through me" (John 14:6). As Christians who have confessed belief in Jesus, we are led by Christ into the presence of the Father. We are also given the Holy Spirit to dwell within us. The Holy Spirit in us is proof of God's presence. Galatians 5:22-23 tells us, "The fruit of the Spirit is love, joy, peace, forbearance, kindness, goodness, faithfulness, gentleness and self-control." By virtue of the Holy Spirit's indwelling, we have access to love and joy and so much more.

Scripture confirms that God gives good gifts to His children and that "every good and perfect gift is from above, coming down from the Father of the heavenly lights, who does not change like shifting shadows" (James 1:17).

When we have accepted Jesus as our Savior, have been led to the Father and have the Spirit living in us, we are disciples of Christ and can claim our freedom in Christ. Jesus said, "If you hold to my teaching, you are really my disciples. Then you will know the truth, and the truth will set you free" (John 8:31-32).

As I let Scripture wash over me, I felt a deeper appreciation for the experience of joy and grew to marvel at how its opposite served to make my appreciation all the more intense. Perhaps you too have noticed how trials intensify your gratitude for moments of joy. Mia's trials are necessarily my trials. And it is precisely because of these trials that my definition of joy has vastly changed from one dependent on circumstances to one dependent on the presence of God. I look forward to exploring this truth with you throughout Study Nine.

My prayer is that we will all experience greater freedom by the truth of Christ for a renewed experience of God-gifted joy.

9.2: God's Joy Has No Barriers

The world offers us ample ammunition with which to fend off God's gift of joy. As I shared in the reading for 9.1, I have been tempted to take the world's bait only to discover that it leads to destruction, NOT relief and NOT healing. When Mia was diagnosed in the hospital emergency room at 3 a.m. with significant brain malformation, my youngest daughter, then six, could not stop laughing. I was in shock, my husband tongue-tied, and my older girls somber, yet my little one giggled on. When my husband recovered enough to ask her if she understood what was happening, she said, "Yes Daddy, I understand, but if I don't laugh, I will cry!"

It took me sometime to understand the wisdom from the mouth of my babe, but I came to see there is no way around this—it is indeed our choice, to laugh or cry at every turn. I imagine we have all found ourselves laughing so hard that we begin to cry. Is it possible then to cry so hard that we begin to laugh? I have found it is indeed a powerful antidote for life with Mia.

**Take a minute to make a list of all the circumstances and people
who have tempted you, or could tempt you, away from the joy
God calls you to experience in Him.**

As we have discussed in previous lessons, the Bible is full of stories about the difficult situations and armies of adversaries God's people faced. Yet it is equally full of God's fulfilled promise to fill His people with joy. Below are some highlights from Scripture.

After years of barrenness, Sarah said, "God has brought me laughter, and everyone who hears about this will laugh with me" (Genesis 21:6).

Psalm 126 reflects the joy felt by God's people when they were restored to Jerusalem. Scholars believe this passage refers either to the restoration after 70 years of exile or the miraculous aversion of the Assyrian attack. Their joy is described in verses 1-3:

> When the LORD restored the fortunes of Zion, we were like those who dreamed. Our mouths were filled with laughter, our tongues with songs of joy. Then it was said among the nations, "The LORD has done great things for them. The LORD has done great things for us, and we are filled with joy.

And amidst the many trials of Job, including the loss of his fortune, his family, and his health, we read, "He will yet fill your mouth with laughter and your lips with shouts of joy" (Job 8:21).

*He will yet fill your
mouth with laughter
and your lips with
shouts of joy.
Job 8:21*

While my young daughter prophesied about the need for joy when faced with tragedy, the state of shock I experienced upon hearing Mia's initial diagnosis of brain malformation led the hospital staff to admit me to a room of my own—with a team of nurses in attendance. I am not sure to this day how long I was in that room, but it lingers with me still as having felt like forever to my rattled mind. When I recovered enough to function, I wandered the halls in disbelief that anyone in that hospital could smile or laugh.

After several weeks in the hospital with Mia, I wrote a piece of prose called the "Merry Band." Below is an excerpt:

We have no choice, we parents of the labeled ones
we must form a merry band or be crushed by our sorrows
For because we feel pain so often, so deeply
we must also learn to feel delight, more often, more deeply
We simply must learn to explode
bent over double with laughter, snorts, giggles
lest we implode with grief

While I became convinced in those first grueling hospital weeks that I needed to find joy again, I also knew I was incapable of doing so on my own. I needed God to show me the way. His method of helping me fully appreciate the godly joy I had so long prayed for was to entrust me with the care of His little Mia. Consider the verses below.

If you, then, though you are evil, know how to give good gifts
to your children, how much more will your Father in heaven
give good gifts to those who ask him!
Matthew 7:11

Children are a heritage from the LORD, offspring a reward from him.
Like arrows in the hands of a warrior are children born in one's youth.
Blessed is the man whose quiver is full of them.
Psalm 127:3-5

God only gives good gifts to His children.

God only gives good gifts to His children. We are His children. And our children are His gifts to us. While I would never advocate that Mia's disabilities are "good," I do know that she is my good gift from God. Whenever I have found cause to doubt, He has been faithful to reassure me in so very many ways.

When you find yourself doubting the goodness of God's gifts to you, ask the Holy Spirit to open your eyes more fully, especially as this may relate to the goodness of the gift of your child. Ask Him to help you come to a deeper appreciation of joy's role in your relationship with your child.

9.3: The Gift of Laughter

A joyful heart is good medicine, but a crushed spirit dries up the bones.
Proverbs 17:22

Living with a crushed heart can become a way of life for the parent of a disabled child. The world nods its head in sympathetic understanding of our pain and seems to condone our distressed state. To avoid falling prey to our strangled hearts, we need to actively seek ways to chuckle at ourselves, especially when we are caught in the "poor haggard parent of a special needs child" persona.

Relate a time you felt like you were wearing your heartbroken parent persona on your sleeve.

I remember a time when a friend and I were attending a small group meeting for parents of children with autism. We were not familiar with the meeting location and thus did not know what entrance to use in this large church. As we were debating this in the parking lot, we spied a group of people at the far end of the lot. They were talking loudly and throwing their heads back in laughter, my friend and I looked at each other, "Not our group," we both said in unison. Then we saw another smaller group of people, their shoulders a bit hunched and they spoke in soft, tired voices, "Ah, there is our group," we chuckled.

Once in the meeting room, we shared our story and every one of us took that opportunity to laugh at ourselves because we each realized that we often wear our trials like they are the whole of who we are and all of what we experience in life. We spent that meeting discussing the fact that we each actually did have some joy in our lives. And we each acknowledged that along with challenges, life also kept offering up beauty and laughter.

> **Even in the midst of a difficult time, have you ever found yourself moved to laughter? What led to this emotional transition?**

Humor is a great release when we contemplate our child's past or probable behaviors. When we first put Mia in school, she was nearly 8. For her previous years, we had managed a "round-the-clock" home therapy program. Our goal was to curb the difficult behaviors of our unpredictable, nonverbal, and aggressive child so that she could participate meaningfully in society. We also sought to teach her language, useful social interaction, and proficient gross and fine motor skills.

When the possibility that she could be ready for school dawned on us, we were tentatively hopeful. We knew she was a seesawing mix of sweet and sour, but we did not know if anyone outside our home therapy program would be able to see beyond the sour to appreciate the sweet. So, on that first day of school,

I dressed Mia as cute as a button, hoping her adorably impish looks would steal her teachers' hearts long before her completely inappropriate behaviors stole their sanity.

I brought Mia into the multiage inclusion classroom on that first day of school, and as I had anticipated, she got that initial "AWW, she is adorable!" from her teachers. In fact, all five of her teachers quite immediately fell in love with her angelic features. I knew they were hooked by love at first sight, but I also knew the next few hours would show them another side of my angel.

When I picked her up, the teachers described to me that between her hugs, "I love yous," and imaginative nicknames for her teachers, she had stripped off all her clothing, run naked out of the bathroom, kicked one of her teachers in the face (breaking her glasses) and bopped a girl in a neighboring classroom on the head. My choice—horror or mirth. For self-preservation I chose mirth and, lucky for me, her teachers did as well.

The Holy Spirit was at work in that classroom and busily so, because those teachers joyfully invited Mia to become a permanent part of that classroom. God bless them each. They chose to look at my child as a challenge worth taking—a challenge full of amazing and joy-filled rewards!

> **Do you have humorous or heartwarming stories that center around your child's disability? If so, share one below.**

9.4: Cultivating Laughter

Increased laughter is a joy we can cultivate in our lives. One way to do this is through the activities we choose for entertainment and the people we choose for company. I love funny shows, movies, books, and I am drawn to people who make me laugh. One couple I have been particularly close to has a child diagnosed with cerebral palsy, epilepsy, and anxiety. They make it a regular part of their routine to catch local and visiting comedians as often as possible both on TV and around town.

Taking their cue, I have found my own source of comic relief in hanging out with neurotypical children and observing their perspectives on Mia. It never fails to prove a hilarious experience. On one occasion, my 10-year-old neighbor, Cydney, told me about a conversation she had with one of her friends in which the friend, while observing Mia, said "I think I have what Mia has." Cydney, who had known Mia almost all her life, strongly disagreed, but her friend insisted saying, "No, really, I think I have autopsy!" Mia, who could outlast the energizer bunny at every turn, is hardly an autopsy candidate, but I often wish I could get inside her little body and understand just how her jumbled up nervous system operates.

On another occasion, Mia was at the pool and ran by two little boys, hitting one of them as she sped by. One of the boys was familiar with Mia's impulsive behaviors, but the boy who was hit did not know Mia. He looked quizzically at his friend with an expression of, "What's up with that?" His friend brushed off the event saying, "Oh that's just Mia, she's authentic!" And indeed, you can find no more authentic girl in town!

Why do you suppose God gave us the ability to laugh? Why is laughter important?

The one enthroned in heaven laughs.
Psalm 2:4

I have found that the funny, nonchalant things kids say are a great antidote for despair. God made a beautiful world and has the power to turn every heartache into something extraordinary. He also created a funny world with many odd creatures. I find my Mia to be among God's oddest.

Psalm 2:4 is one of my favorite and often referred to verses for it ascribes to God a sense of humor, "The one enthroned in heaven laughs." In my imaginings, God has a deep and hardy laugh, and I believe if He can find things to laugh about in this world of heartbreak, certainly He will empower us to do so as well.

Take some time to reflect on what you can do in your life to cultivate more laughter for yourself and your family. Write your thoughts below.

9.5: Oil and Water

Joy would seem to be the opposite of suffering, like oil and water, the two do not intuitively mix. Yet one of the most beautiful and intimate letters written by Paul, the letter to the Philippians, seems to call us to just this unlikely mix.

Paul writes:

> I want you to know, brothers and sisters, that what has
> happened to me has actually served to advance the gospel.
> As a result, it has become clear throughout the whole palace
> guard and to everyone else that I am in chains for Christ.
> And because of my chains, most of the brothers and sisters
> have become confident in the Lord and dare all the more to
> proclaim the gospel without fear…The important thing is
> that in every way…Christ is preached. And because of this
> I rejoice. Yes, and I will continue to rejoice, for I know that
> through your prayers and God's provision of the Spirit of Jesus
> Christ what has happened to me will turn out for my deliverance.
> **Philippians 1:12-14, 18-19**

Paul writes to his beloved Philippians while he is in the midst of exceptional suffering, yet he claims to have joy because of the suffering! His imprisonment has led to the spread of the gospel and furthermore has even hastened its expansion. Paul points to the knowledge and spread of God's truth as his source of joy. He rejoices in eternal life with God where unfathomable goodness abounds as his cause for joy.

The gospel truth offers all believers a joy that walks hand in hand with suffering.

Penning his convictions with eloquence, Paul shares the gospel truth that offers all believers a joy that walks hand in hand with suffering. He is quite clearly advising his beloved church members to rejoice, not despite their sufferings, but in their sufferings. How is this possible?

Have you ever rejoiced in the soreness you feel after a good workout because you know the physical results will be wonderful? Have you ever gloried over long hours spent on an important career project because you knew the financial rewards would be fabulous? Have you ever recounted the pains of childbirth with tender fondness because the precious child in your arms was worth every contraction and push? Have you ever taken on the taxing and emotional draining task of caring for a loved one as they made their way toward heaven because you knew those priceless tender moments of devoted love will last into eternity? And have you ever fought through the heartbreak of redirecting a wayward child because you knew that, right along with you, all of heaven rejoices over one lost soul who finds the way home?

Take a minute and recall some difficult things you have endured for the joy they had in store.

We endure much trial for the joy set before us, and when we do we are imitators of Christ who, "For the joy set before him he endured the cross, scorning its shame, and sat down at the right hand of the throne of God" (Hebrews 12:2).

Anyone can believe in God; it takes real faith to believe God.
Dr. R.C. Sproul

The real strength of our belief, and consequently our capacity for joy, is tested by whether we believe what God tells us through His Word. As Dr. R.C. Sproul was known for saying, "Anyone can believe in God; it takes real faith to believe God."

Do you believe not only that God exists, but also that He will act in your life according to His good promises in Scripture? Do you believe He has set joy before you?

As I worked on this study, the mother of my daughter's college roommate was diagnosed with terminal cancer. She entered hospice, and her daughter journaled on Caringbridge.com to allow friends and family to keep up with her progress toward heaven. In one entry, her daughter quoted these words by Ann Voskamp,

> Joy and pain, they are but two arteries of the one heart that pumps through all those who don't numb themselves to really living—and the way through the pain is to reach out to others in theirs. Use me today, and let me become the gift back to You through the work before me. In thanks for all Your gifts, make me a gift, because becoming the blessing is what deeply blesses. Enter into me, even me, and use my life to be Your love. This I pray. Amen.

This is a truly beautiful prayer that I identify with in so many ways. I have found the terror and angst Mia's diagnosis causes to be unbearable at times, yet she also gives us ample opportunity to laugh deeply and experience tender joy. It is as if the deeper our pain has gone, so too has our joy been deepened. As parents of special needs children, we are not alone in facing heartbreak. The world is overrun with unfathomable pain, grief, and horror, perhaps against the backdrop of someone else's tribulations, our trials pale. Yet wherever our challenges fall on the relative scale of pain, we all have the same promise from above—we have joy set before us!

This promise was actualized sevenfold for me when I mustered up the courage to turn my pain into an opportunity to reach out to others with compassion and hope. I encourage you to set your pain before the Lord and wait expectantly for He is faithful to His Word. He will transform it into joy beyond your expectations.

Small Group Discussion

Study Nine - In Christ We Can Know Complete Joy

After you have individually reviewed the readings and reflection questions, meet with your small group using the suggested format below:

Believe: Christ has called us to joy!

Scripture Reading: What does this verse mean to you?

> Rejoice in the Lord always. I will say it again: Rejoice!
> **Philippians 4:4**

Engage: Review the questions below and allow each person to participate in the discussion.

9.1
- **(1) What is your current definition of joy?**

- **(2) What stands out to you as the source and reason for Christian joy? Consider the verses in John 15:9-11 and Philippians 4:4 in your discussion.**

9.2
- **(3) How have people or circumstances tempted you away from your joy?**

- **(4) What is joy's role in your relationship with your child?**

9.3
- **(5) Relate a time you were wearing your heartbroken parent persona on your sleeve.**

- **(6) Share moments you found yourself moved to laughter in the midst of a difficult time.**

- **(7) What humorous or heartwarming stories that center on your child's disability can you share?**

9.4
- **(8) Why is laughter important?**

- **(9) Share ideas about what you might do to cultivate more laughter for your family and yourself?**

(10) Recount some difficult things you endured for the joy they had in store.

9.5

(11) Along with believing that God exists, why is it also important to believe He will act in your life according to His good promises in Scripture?

(12) Do you believe God has set joy before you? If so how has He proven faithful to bring you joy?

Celebrate: God's presence is our great source of joy. In Him, we can remove all barriers to joy. God gave us laughter and the capacity to give laughter to others. We can actively bring more laughter into our lives. Pain and joy are not mutually exclusive, we can rejoice because of our suffering, for we have joy set before us.

Pray: *Lord, thank You for considering relationship with us Your joy and for setting the joy of relationship with You before us! With You, we can know joy in suffering. We can choose joy and more joy being both receiver and bearer of full on godly laughter. Amen.*

(Add personal petitions and revelation from discussion points.)

This is what the Sovereign LORD,
the Holy One of Israel, says: "In
repentance and rest is your salvation,
in quietness and trust is your strength,
but you would have none of it."
Isaiah 30:15

The One in Charge Is the Ultimate Recharger

Recharge for the Ride

No one can ride a roller coaster indefinitely. At some point, for some length of time, we must get off the roller coaster and leave the amusement park surrounding it. It may be for an evening, a day, a week, a month, or a season—but one thing is clear, time off to clean up, fix up, and recharge is always in order.

In the same way, few of us have the stamina to be the sole caregiver of our special needs child 24/7—it's a yoke entirely too heavy for one person to bear alone. Yet, sometimes in our quest to help our children, we behave like the Israelites God referred to in Isaiah 30:15 and turn down the rest God offers us. I have found it is crucial to keep in mind that while being a "parent to a special needs child" is one very important role we play in life, we also play many other roles throughout our days. In fact, there is only one place in which we can move beyond all the roles we play in life. I love how the words of Jesus in Matthew 6 express this in the interpretation of The Message:

> Find a quiet, secluded place so you won't be tempted to role-play before God.
> Just be there as simply and honestly as you can manage. The focus will
> shift from you to God, and you will begin to sense his grace.
> **Matthew 6:6**

Jesus often withdrew to a quiet place to recharge and seek guidance for his ministry. When I read passages about Jesus retiring to a place by Himself to pray, I get a very vivid visual. I imagine Christ bundled up against a bitter earthly cold and as He walks to His place of prayer, I imagine the hat, the mittens, the boots, the coat, the scarf all coming off until he stands in white summer linen before the warmth of His Father. I imagine there, He is refreshed by the loving, guiding presence of His Father. As He leaves this time of prayer, I envision Him picking up each garment, like pieces of His ministerial robe, with renewed joy and purpose as He makes His way back to the rich meaning of His earthly life.

Most Christians who have spent time in God's Word could make a pretty lengthy list of the roles Jesus played. Some of the descriptions of the roles given to Christ found in Scripture include the following:

Son of God, Image of the invisible God, God, Member of the Trinity, Son of Mary and Joseph, Descendant of the House of David, Galilean, Hebrew, Jew, Carpenter, Reformer, Revolutionary, Moralist, Friend to the Friendless, Miracle Worker, Healer, Teacher, Prophet, Revealer of Hearts, A Light in the Darkness, The Resurrected Lord, Great Physician, Conqueror of Death, Captain of the Angels, Prince of Peace, Lamb of God, Our Blessed Hope, Bread of life, Good Shepard, Light of the World, Door of the Sheep, The Way, The Truth, The Life, The True Vine, Jesus of Nazareth, Advocate, Intercessor, Friend, Savior.

We too play many roles in our lives. Examining those roles from several vantage points may provide insight into God's call on our lives—and, thus, how we spend our time.

Study Ten – The One in Charge Is the Ultimate Recharger

10.1: Permission Granted!

While "parent of a special needs child" is one of the roles we play, and certainly a very important one, it is not the entire definition of who we are called to be. We may at times behave as if this role completely defines us and we may even feel like it has consumed us. The reality, however, is that we all shift hats many times over a day, a year, a lifetime.

List the many roles you play beyond parenting your child.

I imagine the roles you listed are as varied as my own. I find myself constantly weighing my many roles and what is required of me in each role against what I need to practice in order to be able to fully function in these capacities. It can be a tricky task for the position we all strive toward is the subtle stabilization of the teeter-totter called BALANCE.

Jesus' primary form of reenergizing was retiring physically to be alone with His Father. To better fulfill His many roles, He often appeared to be stepping away from those roles to spend time in solitary prayer with His Father. Yet, this very act of stepping away allowed Him to more fully fulfill His mission. In fact, He never stopped being any of the crucial things He needed to be to fulfill His earthly mission, because He had a method of reenergizing to live out those roles to the fullest.

Jesus' primary form of reenergizing was retiring physically to be alone with His Father.

It is important to understand that God, in this same way, gives you permission to experience life outside your role as "parent to a special needs child" specifically so that you receive the strength to better fulfill that role. He understands the value of stepping away to reenergize—after all, as I hope you will see in this study, He embodies this very idea.

Read the Scripture below and note Jesus' message to His followers in this passage.

> Then, because so many people were coming and going that they
> did not even have a chance to eat, he said to them, "Come with me by
> yourselves to a quiet place and get some rest." So they went away
> by themselves in a boat to a solitary place.
> **Mark 6:31-32**

Have you ever felt God calling you to come away to rest for a bit? Do you believe He intends for you to do so?

In Mark 12:29, when a scribe asks Jesus which is the most important command of all, He starts His answer like this:

> The most important one is this:
> 'Hear, O Israel: The Lord our God, the Lord is one.

Yet even as one God, the members of the Trinity—Father, Son and Spirit—have different roles and different experiences that make up the One and enrich the manner in which God acts as, and experiences, being God. We can delineate roles of God to include Creator, Judge, Advocate, Guide, Miracle Worker, and Savior.

So, too, even in our humanity we are made in the image of God such that we individually find we are one person with many roles. We have roles of parent, provider, advocate, spouse, sibling, child, cousin, friend, etc. As we manage these roles, we can ask for God's help in the harmonious coexistent, wise separation, and appropriate comingling of our roles.

When we make time to play some of our favorite roles—artist, chef, business person, writer, socialite, athlete, neighbor, parent to our other children, etc.— we better equip ourselves for the roles we must play in order to fulfill the very specific and often struggle-filled parts God has assigned to us. These may be roles we would never have chosen for ourselves, but are clearly roles God wants to equip us to handle with grace.

> **Are there any roles/activities you especially enjoy in which you feel you no longer have time to participate? If so, list those roles and briefly explain what you believe is preventing you from engaging in them.**

Examine your list with care. Use the eyes of the Spirit to help you determine whether these are roles you should strive to find time to play. If you know you are tapped out on special needs parenting and need to spend time in other roles but are not sure what these might be, explore the possibilities with godly intent.

I have found that Mia is just one part of the family, one part of my life. It has been crucial for me to have places for peace to do things that really fill me so that I then have the strength to fill my daughter; but not only to fill my daughter, but also to be filled in the very parenting of her.

God does not ask us to do this parenting job all on our own. He expects us to take time off, and He expects us to give our spouse and other caregivers time off as well. In caring for Mia, we have been blessed with the abilities and help of a team of caregivers. From our older daughters to hired caregivers and therapists, we all rotate responsibility to be sure all caregivers stay fully engaged and able to handle their respective Mia-hours with joy. We all need to cultivate partnerships in caring for our children. If we do not, we may very well end up exhausting ourselves right out of the crucial roles God wants us to play.

I have found the fastest way to spiral down into "copelessness" is to say to myself, How will I do this for the rest of my life? The truth is, we have no idea what the future entails. And we most certainly do not have to do any one thing every second for the rest of our lives. We have choices. Our children will spend time with teachers, therapists, spouses, relatives, caregivers, and, praise the Lord, sleeping! We will have a life outside our child's issues, and we need to keep sight of that. No difficult situation must be endured forever or constantly.

As we have already touched on, the Bible says, "And the God of all grace, who called you to his eternal glory in Christ, after you have suffered a little while, will himself restore you and make you strong, firm and steadfast" (1 Peter 5:10). We can count on this trustworthy verse because we can count on the constancy and reliability of our God.

10.2: Preparing to Play Our Roles

We have identified some roles we play and roles we might like to play. We have asked the Holy Spirit to guide us in determining which roles serve God's good purpose for our lives. Now the task before us is to determine how to allocate our time to the important roles we have identified.

> **Think about how you work toward achieving balance among the many roles you play or wish to play and jot your thoughts below.**

If time with God in prayer and Scripture study is a big part of your balancing act, you can be firmly confident that you will never totter long beyond the boundaries of God's plan. When we make room for God, the tight wire we all walk becomes a wider, firmer foundation. Walking in prayer is faithfully walking the beautiful path of Christ.

Scripture hands us a powerful legacy of Christ's example. Take some time to locate each Scripture below and note what was going on right before each verse or what Jesus was preparing to do. I have done the first one for you.

Matthew 14:23: "After he had dismissed them, he went up on a mountainside by himself to pray. Later that night, he was there alone."

Jesus has just: heard the news of John the Baptist's beheading. He had also healed and fed a multitude with food and the Word in a desert place.

Mark 1:35: "Very early in the morning, while it was still dark, Jesus got up, left the house and went off to a solitary place, where he prayed."

Jesus has just:

Mark 14:32-35: "They went to a place called Gethsemane, and Jesus said to his disciples, 'Sit here while I pray.' He took Peter, James and John along with him, and he began to be deeply distressed and troubled. 'My soul is overwhelmed with sorrow to the point of death,' he said to them. 'Stay here and keep watch.' Going a little farther, he fell to the ground and prayed that if possible the hour might pass from him."

Jesus was preparing to:

If you would like to look at other examples of Christ in prayer, read Luke 5:16, Luke 6:12, Luke 9:29, Luke 22:41-43 and write out one or two of these verses below.

Do you have a routine ritual you engage in before or after a difficult task? And if every day is difficult, how do you prepare?

Prayer is a powerful way to embrace both the joys and trials of life.

Prayer is a powerful way to embrace both the joys and trials of life. You have no better confidant and counselor than God Almighty. Ask Him to enhance your prayer life and be prepared to experience knee-bending mercy.

10.3: Put on Your Own Mask First

Prayer is an important tool we can use to balance and prioritize our roles. I am sure you are familiar with the airline instructions regarding loss of oxygen on a plane. They say, "Before assisting a child or someone sitting next to you, put on your own mask first." This is wise advice because if you don't get your own mask on first, you may run out of breath in the middle of helping someone else. You may even totally pass out.

The same idea applies to prayer. We must cover our lives and the lives of those around us in prayer. When we are steeped in prayer, literally breathing in conversation with the Lord, we are prepared for anything and we can wield the power of the Word to breathe life into others. Regular, daily conversation with God is meant to be a constant in our lives for this very reason.

When balancing our roles, God can provide great clarity. He has uniquely created us to gravitate toward, have an aptitude for, relax during, and derive energy from, specific God-gifted activities. It is important that we find a balanced way to engage in these renewing pleasures, a way that balances respect for our family's needs and our own. God designed us with unique propensities to find relaxation and rejuvenation in the good things of this world. His Word references rest in many places. Let's start by looking at Genesis.

After God created the world, what did He do? You most likely have a ready answer, but take the time to read Genesis with fresh eyes and a Spirit-led heart and fill in the blanks below:

Thus the heavens and the earth were completed in all their vast array. By the seventh day God had finished the work he had been doing; so on the seventh day he _____ from all his work. Then God blessed the seventh day and made it holy, because on it he _____ from all the work of creating that he had done.
Genesis 2:1-3

This passage tells us that rest is so important to God that He blessed and made "holy" a full day of it! And He went even further: He not only took this day off, but He also instructs us to take a day off every single week saying:

Rest is so important to God that He blessed and made "holy" a full day of it!

Six days you shall labor, but on the seventh day you shall rest;
even during the plowing season and harvest you must rest.
Exodus 34:21

What an amazingly good God we serve. He does not begrudge or stingily dole out 15-minute breaks here and there, nor does He barter and quibble about a day of vacation. Rather He ordains an entire day of rest every week. That's 52 God-ordained days of rest a year! God knows what His children need.

But here is an interesting twist, Scripture also tells us that God never rests or tires. Isaiah 40:28 says, "Do you not know? Have you not heard? The LORD is the everlasting God, the Creator of the ends of the earth. He will not grow tired or weary, and his understanding no one can fathom." And further Psalm 121:1-4 says, "My help comes from the LORD, the Maker of heaven and earth. He will not let your foot slip—he who watches over you will not slumber; indeed, he who watches over Israel will neither slumber nor sleep."

So, it is clear God rests while at the same time never tiring from work. Perhaps then, the meaning of the Sabbath rest might be more akin to a sense of reflection and fulfilled satisfaction—a sense of a job truly well done. This definition offers us the possibility of resting amidst any situation in which we find ourselves, because we know God has us covered.

Spend some time in prayer and ask the Lord to help you come to a deeper understanding of the rest He is calling you to experience. Then write out your own definition of what it means for you personally to experience the rest of God.

10.4: Enter Into His Rest

We have seen from the Scripture study in 10.3 that rest is a biblically ordained experience. Yet, I wonder if you, like me, find yourself working on every God-ordained day of rest. After all, we play the role of parents to special needs children and so many other roles as well. If you find yourself in this situation too, fear not, we are in good company. Christ was a healer; this was part of the good work He was anointed to do. It was part of His job description.

> You know what has happened, throughout the province of Judea,
> beginning in Galilee after the baptism that John preached-how God
> anointed Jesus of Nazareth with the Holy Spirit and power,
> and how he went around doing good and healing all who were under
> the power of the devil, because God was with him.
> **Acts 10:37-38**

Jesus did this work even on the Sabbath and was soundly condemned by the Pharisees for doing so. Mark 3:1-5 tells us of one such Sabbath:

> Another time Jesus went into the synagogue, and a man with a shriveled
> hand was there. Some of them were looking for a reason to accuse Jesus,
> so they watched him closely to see if he would heal him on the Sabbath.
> Jesus said to the man with the shriveled hand, "Stand up in front of
> everyone." Then Jesus asked them, "Which is lawful on the Sabbath:
> to do good or to do evil, to save life or to kill?" But they remained silent.
> He looked around at them in anger and, deeply distressed at their
> stubborn hearts, said to the man, "Stretch out your hand."
> He stretched it out, and his hand was restored.

Jesus healed this man on the Jewish day of rest, the day on which the Jewish leaders were convinced no work of any kind was to be done.

Since Christ tells us in Matthew 5:17, "Do not think that I have come to abolish the Law or the Prophets; I have not come to abolish them but to fulfill them," surely there is some scriptural explanation for His actions. The letter to the Hebrews sheds some light on this for me, and I love how The Message interprets this passage from Hebrews 4:1-3:

> For as long, then, as that promise of resting in him pulls us on to God's
> goal for us, we need to be careful that we're not disqualified. We received
> the same promises as those people in the wilderness, but the promises
> didn't do them a bit of good because they didn't receive the promises with
> faith. If we believe, though, we'll experience that state of resting.

This passage instructs us that we have the same promise of freedom and rest that God gave the Israelites when He powerfully released them from captivity. Yet it also cautions us that because the Israelites did not believe God's promise they wound up wandering the desert for 40 years. I am sure you, like me, would prefer not to wander a desert for any extended length of time. So how do we harness our belief to experience God's rest?

My Presence will go with you, and I will give you rest.
Exodus 33:14

In Exodus, God says, "My Presence will go with you, and I will give you rest" (Exodus 33:14). Christ further shed His ministerial light on this exact question when He says: "Come to me, all you who are weary and burdened, and I will give you rest. Take my yoke upon you and learn from me, for I am gentle and humble in heart, and you will find rest for your souls. For my yoke is easy and my burden is light" (Matthew 11:28-30).

The key to our rest is experiencing the presence of the Lord. We must build a daily relationship with Christ, because He designed each of us to find true rest in communing with Him. As we studied in the 10.2 reading, this is exactly how Christ rested—in refreshing communion with His Father. We foster a relationship with God when we read, study, and pray His Word.

God's Word gives us fresh strength, hope, skill, and courage to tackle the challenges ahead of us and to greet each day with a commitment to live with appreciative God-focused eyes. When we take our concerns and our praise to Him, we deepen this relationship, and He gives us rest.

Scripture is full of the promise we have of rest in the Lord. Let the truth of these verses bring you into the rest of Christ.

In vain you rise early and stay up late, toiling for food to eat—
for he grants sleep to those he loves.
Psalm 127:2

I will refresh the weary soul, and satisfy the faint.
Jeremiah 31:25

Blessed is the one you discipline, LORD, the one you teach
from your law; you grant them relief from days of trouble.
Psalm 94:12-13

The LORD is my shepherd, I lack nothing. He makes me lie down
in green pastures, he leads me beside quiet waters, he refreshes
my soul. He guides me along the right paths for his name's sake.
Even though I walk through the darkest valley, I will fear no evil,
for you are with me; your rod and your staff, they comfort me.
You prepare a table before me in the presence of my enemies.
You anoint my head with oil; my cup overflows.
Psalm 23:1-5

Better one handful with tranquility than two
handfuls with toil and chasing after the wind.
Ecclesiastes 4:6

> **The key to our rest is experiencing the presence of the Lord.**

> Relate an experience when your awareness of God's presence
> and/or your knowledge of His Word gave you rest while dealing
> with a daunting or challenging situation.

10.5: Wrestling for Your Rest

Often, learning to accept a troubling situation or role we find ourselves in, and coming to understand God's intention for us in that situation or role, lands us in a wrestling match with God. It can take the form of desperate repetitive pleas to God for a mental understanding of "Why me?" or it can take the form of what feels like a true physical wrestling match. Before Jacob returned to face the brother he had cheated out of his birthright, Genesis 32 speaks about Jacob's wrestling match with God.

> So Jacob was left alone, and a man wrestled with him
> till daybreak. When the man saw that he could not overpower him,
> he touched the socket of Jacob's hip so that his hip was wrenched
> as he wrestled with the man. Then the man said,
> "Let me go, for it is daybreak."
> **Genesis 32:24-26**

Jacob feared for his life and he feared he might lack the courage to live as the changed man God was calling him to be. His fears, like our own, were very real to him. Jacob took His fears to the Lord and wrestled with trusting God to help him move forward versus acting on his human instinct to retreat.

> As the parent of a special needs child, I wrestle with exhaustion,
> frustration, fear, sorrow, and isolation. What misgivings or fears
> do you wrestle with in raising your child?

Jacob was wrestling with uncertainty regarding how his brother would receive him. He desperately needed assurance that all would be well if he rode to meet the brother he'd wronged. Thus, he refused to let God go saying, "I will not let you go unless you bless me" (Genesis 32:26).

Jacob was determined to stay locked in spiritual warrior-like prayer as long as it took. He was holding on to God for dear life. At long last, his blessing of peace was achieved through complete trust in the Lord—complete surrender. To commemorate the struggle's outcome, God gave him a new name:

> "What is your name?" "Jacob," he answered. Then the man said, "Your name will no longer be Jacob, but Israel because you have struggled with God and with humans and have overcome." Jacob said, "Please tell me your name." But he replied, "Why do you ask my name?" Then he blessed him there. So Jacob called the place Peniel, saying, "It is because I saw God face to face, and yet my life was spared." The sun rose above him as he passed Peniel, and he was limping because of his hip.
> **Genesis 32:27-31**

Jacob received his new name of strength and promise. He received his peace and he also bore the scar of the battle—a limp. Now a limp might signify to some a weakness, but in God's economy that limp would forever signify the gift of God's strength to overcome fears and failures.

What are some of your scar-like reminders of your wrestling matches with God?

We each have our own battle scars. Mia is one of mine. When Mia was first diagnosed, a friend asked if I had considered putting her in a home so we would not have to endure the difficulty of dealing with her all our lives. I had not, and

God made it clear to me this was not His will. Still, I have regularly wrestled with Him in prayer over how to accomplish His will regarding Mia. He has made it abundantly evident to me time and time again, because as I have said, I am indeed a hard-headed woman, that Mia is my sign of strength in battle, of overcoming.

Still, parenting her is a daily chore. It is comforting to me to know I am not alone. Scripture is full of the hard tasks faced by God's people, from Cain, Abraham, Moses, and the wandering Jews to the Judges, kings, prophets, and the apostles. They all struggled to do God's will. Some, like Cain, lost the battle; others were more successful in conquering the flesh and moving in the Spirit.

Even Jesus experienced the human struggle. Scripture tells us:

> We do not have a high priest who is unable to empathize
> with our weaknesses, but we have one who has been tempted
> in every way, just as we are—yet he did not sin.
> **Hebrews 4:15**

And Scripture gives us a heartbreaking look at Christ's most intimate struggle when He prayed for the strength to endure the cross saying, "My Father, if it is possible, may this cup be taken from me. Yet not as I will, but as you will" (Matthew 26:39). Jesus forever wears the scars of His wrestling match. They mark Him as the overcomer of sin and death. He even encouraged the original Doubting Thomas to touch them saying, "Put your finger here; see my hands. Reach out your hand and put it into my side. Stop doubting and believe" (John 20:27). Christ's victorious battle scars served to strengthen Thomas' faith.

My grace is sufficient for you, for my power is made perfect in weakness.
2 Corinthians 12:9

The apostle Paul summarized our plight when he wrote, "We were harassed at every turn—conflicts on the outside, fears within" (2 Corinthians 7:5). In a later passage, God tells Paul something very interesting when he is pleading to have a thorn in his side removed. God tells Paul the thorn serves a purpose. He says, "My grace is sufficient for you, for my power is made perfect in weakness" (2 Corinthians 12:9). This tells me that my own thorns have a purpose. They cause me to call on God, to rely on God, and make me a witness to His power.

When it comes to physical strength, my Mia is a brute. The holes in our walls, the door frames barely on their hinges, the cupboards and drawers hanging at unnatural angles all attest to her power. We have tried all manner of medication and therapies to redirect her unharnessed power. Yet, she remains a cannonball ready to explode. As I cleaned up the debris of one recent explosion, the Spirit convicted me with the question: "What do I do with my unharnessed power?" I have power to deal with Mia's frustrating behaviors in any number of ways. I could abuse this power just as she abuses her power. But God calls me to something higher.

Like the memorial limp Jacob was left with after he overcame the guilt of betraying his brother and the fear that his brother would not forgive him, I have my own memorial injury in Mia's disability. Her disability cripples my plans to live life the way I had planned it all out. Instead I have this completely different life.

We can confidently keep our eyes on Jesus in the struggle, because God is faithful to grant blessings each and every time.

God knew on my own I would have had a hard time realizing the flaws in my plans and giving my life over to Him. Mia helped me learn in the most intimate of ways that I can't go on without God. When the cyclical ups and downs of life with her descend into one long drop, I am sometimes tempted to despair. It is then I wrestle with God. He offers to take my fears away and I foolishly try to hold onto them. I praise Him for coming to the mat with me every time! The truth is when I am crippled, I lean on Him most. Mia is my constant reminder to give it all over to the Lord.

We can confidently keep our eyes on Jesus in the struggle, because God is faithful to grant blessings each and every time. The greatest of these blessings is complete rest in God. He recharges our souls for His glory. He gives us strength and endurance to do the impossible with joy. When we live in Him and trust in Him, we are blessed with His rest.

Small Group Discussion

Study Ten - The One in Charge Is the Ultimate Recharger

After you have individually reviewed the readings and reflection questions, meet with your small group using the suggested format below:

Believe: God will give us rest.

Scripture Reading: What does this verse mean to you?

> In peace I will both lie down and sleep; for you alone,
> Lord, make me dwell in safety.
> **Psalm 4:8**

Engage: Review the questions below and allow each person to participate in the discussion.

10.1

(1) Share some of the many roles you play beyond parenting your child.

(2) Do you believe God intends for you to find time to rest and rejuvenate? If so, why do you believe this?

10.2

(3) What things that you especially enjoyed do you now feel you no longer have time to participate in? What prevents you from participating in these activities or roles?

(4) How do you work to achieve balance among the many roles you play?

(5) What did you notice about the many verses referencing what Christ's preparation and renewal strategy was in the reading from 10.2?

(6) What are the routine rituals you engage in before or after a difficult task?

10.3

(7) After God created the World, what did He do?

(8) What does it mean to you to personally experience the rest of God?

10:4

(9) When have you experienced a challenging time and found your awareness of God's presence and/or your knowledge of His Word gave you rest?

(10) What system could you set up in advance to help you remember to seek God's rest in the midst of a specific difficult situation you find yourself frequently facing?

10:5

(11) What factors surrounding your special needs parenting role do you feel prevent you from experiencing God's rest?

(12) What scars or reminders do you have of your wrestling matches with God?

Celebrate: Praise God that He offers us the power and wisdom to handle with His grace the many responsibilities and roles into which He has called us. He gives us affinities for things that rejuvenate us; chief among them is our relationship with Him. He calls us to "enter into" the rest of His presence and He is up for the wrestling match it may take to keep us there.

Pray: *How amazing are Your provisions Lord. Only You can give us rest in our struggles. You use everything for good. Give us the grace to be instruments of Your peace. Help us to balance the roles You have called us to accept. Keep us in close communion with You always, especially throughout our struggles. And do not let us give up until we have received your blessing. Amen.*

(Add group members insights, petitions or praises)

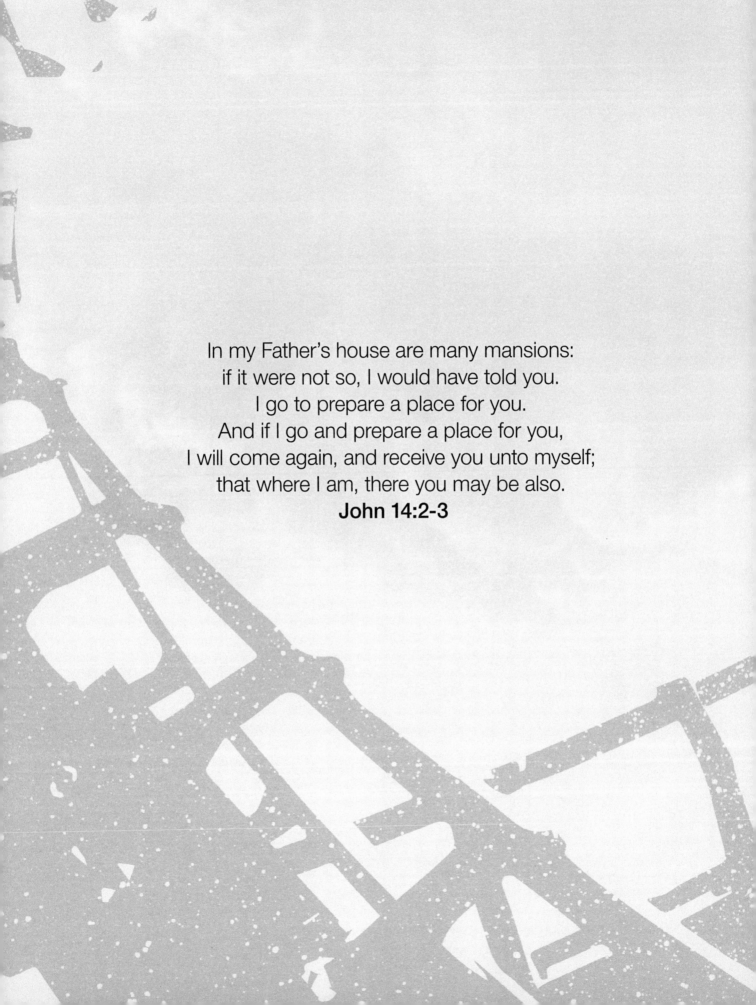

In my Father's house are many mansions:
if it were not so, I would have told you.
I go to prepare a place for you.
And if I go and prepare a place for you,
I will come again, and receive you unto myself;
that where I am, there you may be also.
John 14:2-3

HOME SAVIOR HOME

Focus on Home

In John 14:2-3 Jesus gave a beautiful promise to His disciples. Though they were distraught that He would no longer be with them in the flesh, His promise gave them hope of a great homecoming. Jesus wanted His disciples to understand that He was not abandoning them; rather, He was leaving to make preparations for them to join Him. He promised to come back to the earthly home, which the apostles knew, to take them to the heavenly home He would prepare for them. In the meantime, the apostles were to work out, with the help of His Holy Spirit, how to live in the world without being of the world.

> But very truly I tell you, it is for your good that I am going away.
> Unless I go away, the Advocate will not come to you; but if I go, I will send him to you…
> I have much more to say to you, more than you can now bear. But when he, the Spirit of
> truth, comes, he will guide you into all the truth. He will not speak on his own;
> he will speak only what he hears, and he will tell you what is yet to come.
> **John 16:7, 12-13**

After following Jesus, the apostles' attitudes toward the earth and its people were changed. And after receiving the Holy Spirit, the apostles were ready to take the message Jesus taught them to everyone, everywhere. Jesus departure and the arrival of the Holy Spirit transported the apostles to a new place—a place between seeing Jesus the man, who walked the earth with them, to seeing Jesus the risen Lord, who would welcome them into the glorious paradise He had prepared. What they did in this "in between" place was of great importance, and in John 17, Jesus prayed earnestly to His Father for protection over His disciples as they carried His message of salvation to the world.

> My prayer is not for them alone. I pray also for those who will believe in me through their message, that all of them may be one, Father, just as you are in me and I am in you. May they also be in us so that the world may believe that you have sent me. I have given them the glory that you gave me, that they may be one as we are one—I in them and you in me—so that they may be brought to complete unity. Then the world will know that you sent me and have loved them even as you have loved me. Father, I want those you have given me to be with me where I am, and to see my glory, the glory you have given me because you loved me before the creation of the world.
>
> **John 17:20-24**

Jesus' promises and prayers are for us too as we work out how to live between accepting Jesus as our Savior and seeing Him in paradise. Working out how to live between two points of reference is a common theme for all of us. We work out how to get from each year's beginning to each year's end, from each Monday to Friday, from each sunrise to sunset. We work out how to move from the life we planned for ourselves, to the life we find ourselves living, to the life that awaits us with Christ. We are a people who think and live in the "in between" times.

I began to mull over this concept a bit more when my second daughter attended the University of Georgia and became a committed Bulldog fan. When my husband went up to his first football game at Sanford Stadium, my daughter was beyond thrilled and "instagramed" photos of them in their red, black, and white in front of a sea of similarly dressed fans. Later, my husband recounted his exciting day spent "between the hedges."

The term "between the hedges" is used to reference the location of UGA's stadium because privet hedges have encircled the field since 1929. As every football fan who has ever watched a game at UGA knows, a lot happens "between those hedges." There are all manner of plays that amaze or disappoint from unbelievable passes, exciting sprints toward a touchdown, and glorious wins to disastrous fumbles, injuries, and disheartening defeats. All the drama of an action-packed game is played out before a captivated audience. Yet while Sanford Stadium is called the home of UGA football and is a great place to spend several hours, at the end of the game, every player and every fan departs for a place they consider their truer home.

In reflecting on this, I was struck with the realization that even our truer homes are temporary playing fields, and I began to think of my time on earth as my time "between the trees." On one side are the trees found in the Garden of Eden where all life began and our first home with God was established. On the other side is the tree of life referenced in Revelation.

> Now the LORD God had planted a garden in the east, in Eden; and there he put the
> man he had formed. The LORD God made all kinds of trees grow out of the ground—trees
> that were pleasing to the eye and good for food. In the middle of the garden were the
> tree of life and the tree of the knowledge of good and evil.
>
> **Genesis 2:8-9**

According to Genesis 2:16-17, God told Adam, "You are free to eat from any tree in the garden but you must not eat from the tree of the knowledge of good and evil, for when you eat from it you will certainly die." It is interesting to note that since Adam was created for life, He did not have to eat in order to stay alive. God had created him for life with only one restriction—he was not to eat from "the tree of the knowledge of good and evil," for that would cause him to die. In Genesis 3, we read the story of how Adam and his wife, Eve, took the word of Satan over God's Word and ate the fruit of the forbidden tree. Satan told them they would become like God if they ate it, yet God had told them they would die. When they second-guessed God, they lost access to this wonderful home and were banished from the Garden. God placed "cherubim and a flaming sword flashing back and forth to guard the way to the tree of life" (Genesis 3:24).

The other side of our earthly playing field is the Tree of Life referenced by John the Revelator. In Revelation 22:1-5, John penned:

> Then the angel showed me the river of the water of life, as clear as crystal,
> flowing from the throne of God and of the Lamb down the middle of the great street of
> the city. On each side of the river stood the tree of life, bearing twelve crops of fruit, yielding
> its fruit every month. And the leaves of the tree are for the healing of the nations.
> No longer will there be any curse. The throne of God and of the Lamb will be in the city,
> and his servants will serve him. They will see his face, and his name will be on their
> foreheads. There will be no more night. They will not need the light of a lamp or the light of
> the sun, for the Lord God will give them light. And they will reign for ever and ever.

Did you take note of this tree's remarkable character? It will be on both sides of the river. It will bear twelve kinds of fruits. Its leaves will be healing for the nations. This tree is found in God's paradise city where all things will be made right again. The marvelous Tree of Life will be planted once again "in the midst of the paradise of God" in the new earth where God will give those who do His commandments the "right to the Tree of Life" (Revelation 2:7; 22:14).

> Whoever has ears, let them hear what the Spirit says to the churches. To the one who is
> victorious, I will give the right to eat from the tree of life, which is in the paradise of God.
>
> **Revelation 2:7**

This place among God's trees of life is the amusement park setting of our special needs roller coaster. There are some truly frightening moments and some really thrilling moments, but in every situation the end goal is to ensure all riders make it safely home. In dealing with the entirety of our lives, especially our challenges, our ultimate goal is to move away from pain and toward peace and joy. Scripture tells us there is a place that allows us to do this, a place where there is "no more death or mourning or crying or pain" (Revelation 21:4).

Wouldn't it be wonderful if we could access even a small bit of the peace we will experience when we are raised up to live with Jesus in paradise while we are living among the trees today? As we will see in the readings for Study Eleven, God's Word tells us this is possible. End this day with a prayer that God will help us understand His definition of home!

Study Eleven – Home Savior Home

11.1: A Place Called Home

The idea of home conjures up many images for many people. It is a universal concept, yet it also carries a unique meaning for each person. Webster defines home as: "one's place of residence, the social unit formed by a family living together, a familiar or usual setting, congenial environment; the focus of one's domestic attention." It is also defined as, "a place of origin, an establishment providing residence and care for people with special needs, the objective in various games." To be at home is defined as being "relaxed and comfortable: at ease, in harmony with the surroundings, on familiar ground."

Over the course of Study Eleven, we are going to explore our understanding of the word home. To get us started, make a top-five list of the adjectives you associate with the place you currently call home. Consider whether these adjectives describe a place of comfort or distress.

Home is a central theme in Scripture. From Genesis to Revelation, God talks about His desire to give us a home with Him. He created a home for Adam and Eve. He asked Abraham to travel to a new home of blessing. He promised the freed Israelites He would give them a home of milk and honey. When their errant living caused them to lose that home, He assured the conquered Israelites He would bring them back home. And He committed to His disciples that He is preparing a new and unimaginably glorious home in which we will all join Him.

Look up the verses below and note the importance God places on home.

Genesis 2:8

Genesis 12:1-3

Exodus 3:8:

Jeremiah 29:10-11

1 Corinthians 2:9-10

1 Thessalonians 4:16-18

Clearly, God thinks the idea of home is an important concept. When we go astray, He actively comes looking for us. When we get lost in darkness, He shines His light repeatedly, inviting us to follow His lead to a place of beauty, peace, and glory. When we feel all alone, adrift, and homeless, He lays opportunity for connection and grounding at our feet. The catch is, we must want to be found. We must decide to follow. We must open our hearts and receive His gifts. We must choose to make our home in Him.

Equating home with comfort, goodness, and noteworthiness is an age-old concept. I am sure you are familiar with sayings such as: "Home is where the heart is; feeling completely at home; home plate; homestretch; there is no place like home; keep the home fires burning; home base; nothing to write home about."

Here are a few quotes from people you may recognize about the
idea of home:

- "Love begins by taking care of the closest ones—the ones at home."
  — **Mother Teresa**

- "The strength of a nation derives from the integrity of the home."
  — **Confucius**

- "Home is a place not only of strong affections, but of entire
  unreserve; it is life's undress rehearsal, its backroom, its dressing room."
  —**Harriet Beecher Stowe**

- "I had rather be on my farm than be emperor of the world."
  —**George Washington**

- "There is nothing like staying at home for real comfort."
  —**Jane Austen**

- "Home is a shelter from storms—all sorts of storms."
  —**William J. Bennett**

- "Home is a name, a word, it is a strong one; stronger than magician
  ever spoke, or spirit ever answered to, in the strongest conjuration."
  —**Charles Dickens**

- "The ache for home lives in all of us, the safe place where we can
  go as we are and not be questioned."
  —**Maya Angelou**

- "Where we love is home—home that our feet may leave, but not
  our hearts."
  —**Oliver Wendell Holmes**

Write your own sentence about your concept of the ideal home. If the adjectives you used to describe your current home match what you feel an ideal home should be, then perhaps you might incorporate some of those into your quote.

Compare the quotes on page 203, including your own. Perhaps you will note that the majority of the quotes focus on a specific place. This makes perfect sense to us, the idea of home being a very specific geographical location. Make a list of all the places in your life that have been a physical home to you.

Now make a list of all the places you have ever felt the sense of "being at home" or "I could live here." If your second list includes some of the places you listed above, put a star next to those places. And note if there are any differences in the adjectives you might use to describe the places listed above and below.

As we go through the remaining readings, we will focus on understanding our deep desire for home and creating a God-centered concept of home. I pray our spirits will all be lifted as we delve more deeply into what the Word has to say to us.

11.2: More Than Our Expectations

While for many people, the concept of home conjures up the image of a specific place of coziness, safety, family, and friends, for others, home can mean something they have never experienced or a place they need to get away from as fast as they can. When a place to call home in all the good sense of this concept is unavailable, people often feel disconnected and rootless. And when the safety and delight that we most commonly associate with home is disrupted by very difficult life events, people feel uprooted, or perhaps even think of themselves as living in a broken home.

In a piece called "Smooth and Jagged Treasure," I write about a moment when my oldest daughter was trying to understand how to deal with the way her youngest sister's diagnosis changed our home.

> I find you hiding under tangled hair and shielding arms,
> shoulders shaking in unbearable grief.
> You are mourning the deeply felt loss of comfort upended,
> days sliced thin,
> the two people you most depend upon
> violently propelled to some other dimension,
> far from you.
> The calm of home invaded by tension,
> a minefield of emotions
> that even careful steps
> cause to explode
> in the blinding immediacy of trauma.

Due to Mia's unpredictable seizures and behaviors, home became a place of uncertainty —of waiting for the next shell to drop. I felt like we were caught in a war zone. We never knew what new and frightening symptom each day would bring. We spent our days in hospitals, at the doctors' office, monitoring Mia 24/7. We found ourselves experiencing a deep and painful longing to turn back the hands of time and restore our homelife to pre-Mia diagnosis days.

Mia's trauma was not something we planned into our idea of homelife when we started our family. It wasn't even something we had remotely considered as a possibility. The secure home we had so carefully worked to create was now anything but secure. This was not how we planned it, nor how our lives were supposed to unfold!

While spending a prolonged sojourn in the hospital with Mia, I found I missed many of the simple daily routines of being at home. In those long and wakeful hospital nights, I thought over and over "how comforting to just be home." I wanted to listen to my oldest daughter protest yet another evening of homework, and I vowed I would smile only reassurance. I wanted to referee the ritual rows of my two younger girls over whose turn it was, who touched whom, or some other insurmountable injustice; and I vowed to delight in their melodious voices while mediating their squabbles. I wanted to prepare the sixteen thousand four hundred and twenty-fifth meal of my motherhood decades and wash the two hundred forty-six thousand one hundred and ninety-fifth dish, and I vowed to chop, sauté, bake, serve, soap, rinse, and dry as if I were conducting a symphony. I wanted to make the rounds through my home on tired legs picking up toys, papers, clothes, and pausing to read a story, calm a fear, or indulge in the retelling of a day, and I vowed to dance only pirouettes on those tired legs. I wanted to lie in my own bed next to my husband of many decades, just maybe without a little body wedged between his warmth and mine, and I vowed to feel only newlywed fancy and hope.

I wanted to be back home and enjoy all the homelife moments that perhaps before Mia I had not properly appreciated. I wanted home because home was my safe haven away from the uncertainty of my child's malfunctioning brain and body. The problem was that when I left that hospital, I was going to be taking my little baby time bomb with me. How, with this damaged and damaging child in tow, could home ever again be anything but chaotic, marked with worry, and "comfortless"?

> **Take a moment to consider what aspects of your home and homelife give you a sense of comfort. Then think about how your definition of home as a place of comfort has been, or would be, changed if these things have been, or were, taken from you.**

As an overall concept, most of us generally expect the idea of home to equate to the idea of contentment and happiness. After Mia, I wanted desperately to find a way to restore the happiness that I thought had been torn away from my home. And so my husband and I found ourselves exploring the idea of happiness when we went on a particularly liberating retreat for parents of children with autism.

At this retreat, the presenter asked us why we had each come. We all answered, "We want our kids to be happy!" "Are they happy?" he asked. Then he asked us to close our eyes and visualize our kids when left to their own devices. And what ran through all our heads was that sometimes they are not so happy, just like our typical kids, but other times they are perfectly content—and yet we were still so unhappy, because we view them, even in their contentedness, as in need of our saving.

I understood then that the real issue was our own desperate desire to be happy and our belief that we could not be happy—could not have a happy home—if our child suffered from a disability. It seemed most of the other participants were having the same "aha" moment. And when he asked us again why we were there, we all echoed in unison "Because we want to be happy!"

Our retreat presenter then spoke about how our emotional perspectives can lock us into a state of unhappiness and pain, and he spoke about finding ways to choose happiness by severing the link between circumstances and happiness. You see, the tempo of any home resides in the perspectives of those who live in that home. As the leaders of our home, my husband and I needed to set the example; we needed to set the tone.

Interestingly, as we learned in Study 8, this is a very biblical concept. Paul said:

> I am not saying this because I am in need, for I have learned to be content whatever the circumstances. I know what it is to be in need, and I know what it is to have plenty. I have learned the secret of being content in any and every situation, whether well fed or hungry, whether living in plenty or in want. I can do all this through Him who gives me strength.
> **Philippians 4:11-13**

Are there things you want for your child that seem elusive and are thus having a negative impact on your sense of happiness?

There were many things we wanted for Mia when we went on this retreat. However, as the lesson progressed, our facilitator suggested that we could prioritize goals for our child while maintaining an attitude of wanting these goals to be achieved WITHOUT attaching our happiness to the getting of them. This allowed us to focus on creating contentment as an inner decision versus a set of circumstances. The idea of circumstance-independent contentment was also useful to us in helping Mia's siblings make sense of life with an epileptic and autistic sister. It helped us sympathize with them while encouraging them not to get trapped in endless self-pity. We were able to help them look for the blessings that exist as surely as do the challenges.

We all long for stability. The romanticized ideas of home assign stability as a defining characteristic of "home." However, as Christians and as special needs parents, we are well acquainted with the fact that stability is not always part of the homelife package. Scripture is very clear with us on this point, assuring us we will have troubles in this life.

> For we know that if the earthly tent we live in is destroyed, we have a building from God, an eternal house in heaven, not built by human hands. Meanwhile we groan, longing to be clothed instead with our heavenly dwelling, because when we are clothed, we will not be found naked. For while we are in this tent, we groan and are burdened, because we do not wish to be unclothed but to be clothed instead with our heavenly dwelling, so that what is mortal may be swallowed up by life. Now the one who has fashioned us for this very purpose is God, who has given us the Spirit as a deposit, guaranteeing what is to come.
> **2 Corinthians 5:1-5**

We have an anchor that stabilizes us in this world's wild waters. We have Christ.

Scripture is also very clear that trouble does not rule the day; rather; hope allows us to turn this seemingly hopeless situation on its head because we have an anchor that stabilizes us in this world's wild waters. We have Christ. Our difficult path causes us to more firmly lean on Christ, our only true lasting security. Our hope in Christ and the eternal home He is preparing for us with God is where our definition of home takes root. Remember John 16:33, "In this world you will have trouble. But take heart! I have overcome the world."

11.3: A New Heaven and a New Earth

We have romanticized ideas of what our homes on earth ought to be on one hand, and we have the reality of severely dysfunctional, traumatized, or loveless homes on the other. In between, we have all manner of homelife played out with a mix of wonderful, weird, and woeful. Amidst it all, most people long for home as a place of safety, comfort, and plenty—a place where everybody knows your name and loves you. For Christians, our hope for this kind of home lies in the promises of Scripture.

The Bible tells us we have an eternal home—a home without suffering, or cruelty, or evil of any kind. It is called "a better country—a heavenly one" (Hebrews 11:16), "a city which has foundations, whose builder and maker is God" (Hebrews 11:10), "a paradise" (Luke 23:43).

The Bible tells us we have an eternal home — a home without suffering, or cruelty, or evil of any kind.

Read these verses below and note your reaction about the promises given in these verses.

But in keeping with His promise we are looking forward to a new heaven
and a new earth, where righteousness dwells.
2 Peter 3:13

Notes:

Then I saw "a new heaven and a new earth," for the first heaven and
the first earth had passed away, and there was no longer any sea. I saw
the Holy City, the new Jerusalem, coming down out of heaven from God,
prepared as a bride beautifully dressed for her husband. And I heard
a loud voice from the throne saying, "Look! God's dwelling place is now
among the people, and he will dwell with them. They will be his people,
and God himself will be with them and be their God. 'He will wipe every
tear from their eyes. There will be no more death' or mourning or crying
or pain, for the old order of things has passed away.
Revelation 21:1-4

Notes:

When I read about the beauty, peace, and joy of the new heaven and earth, this human longing for a secure home makes perfect sense to me. God designed us to live in a paradise in perfect relationship with Him. Since the departure from Eden, much of the human race has been living largely outside the design of our maker. Because of this, we experience all manner of dysfunction in this temporary place we call home.

Look up these verses. Then write in your own words what the verses say about our eternal home:

God designed us to live with Him.

Philippians 3:20-21

1 Corinthians 2:9

Revelation 21:10-27

Revelation 7:9-10

Acts 7:55-56

Matthew 8:11

1 Corinthians 13:12

John 14:3

The truth is we were designed to live with glorious bodies in a very real place of unimaginable beauty. This place will have room enough for multitudes. There will be no strangers. We will all recognize each other. We will understand deeply and feel deeply understood. And Jesus will always be there with us.

We pine for this place in ways we can't fully comprehend. Every time we feel like a misfit—alone, awkward, unwanted—we experience spiritual longing for our true home. God designed us to live with Him. Life in His kingdom is the only answer to the longing a human heart has for a truly good home where everything is as we hope, expect, and desire it to be.

11.4: Home Alone

Would the room Jesus prepared for us in our Father's house fit our definition of home if we were there alone? Let's explore this idea a bit by considering the popular comedy Home Alone. The plot revolves around a young boy, Kevin, who is mistakenly left behind when everyone frantically rushes out the door for a family vacation abroad. At first, Kevin is elated to be free of family drama and rules, but eventually his joy turns to fear, and he is overwhelmed with relief and delight when his family finally returns home.

> Take a moment to ponder what you have equated with the idea of being home alone or how you felt when you were momentarily away from home at these various stages of your life.

Home alone as a small child:

Home alone as a teen:

Away from home as a young adult in college or your first job:

Home alone temporarily as an adult:

When I was young, I equated being home alone with hearing strange noises and being afraid to look in the basement. My older sister used to babysit the six of us when my parents went out, and she often put pots and pans in front of all the doors as an alarm system against intruders. If she heard a noise, she would line up six pajama-clad kids behind her and lead us creeping down the stairs to investigate.

As I became a teen, the idea of being home alone meant I could do things my parents might not completely approve of like stay up late, eat in my room, or have a few friends over. I felt a sense of controlling my own destiny, being my own boss, and bending the rules a bit. In retrospect, this was naturally a very immature paradise-view of the situation.

When I was in college, I pined for home. I could not wait to come home for the holidays. My mother always met me at the airport with a box of chocolate covered cherries. She had a cozy bed made up for me, put up with the explosion my suitcase became as my clothes jumped out everywhere upon opening, and then prepared copious delicious meals for me. My father presided over wine-filled meals with tender toasts. And my five younger siblings, especially my youngest brother and sister, were reliably adorable in their affections. My older sister alternated between inspiring me with what she was making of her life and bossing me around—and even the bossing I nostalgically embraced, because going home for the holidays meant going home to hug and enjoy my large family of nine.

Now that I am older, I am rarely in my busy home alone. When I am, I consider it pure bliss. Yet this bliss is predicated on a temporary home-alone experience, and I am always looking forward to the moment the silence is broken by the return of my four daughters and husband.

I bring all of this up to suggest that our definition of home, and the joy we find in it, changes as we mature—similar to the maturation of our faith. Over time the idea of home progresses to mean more than the comforts of a certain location. Rather, home comes to be defined by the people who come and go and the memories created there.

One article I found particularly interesting on this idea was written by a blogger and father of four, David Marine. He writes this:

The English word "home" is from the Old English word hām which actually refers to a village or estate where many "souls" are gathered. It implies there's a physical dwelling involved, but the main idea is that it's a gathering of people. One dictionary I came across online had an interpretation of the modern definition of home that I really like. It states that home is "the abiding place of the affections." To me, that sums it up like nothing else. It's not a building or a room, but a place where your love dwells.

The Latin root word for home is actually the same word we use for human being, person and people. At its very core, home is where not just your heart is, but the hearts of those you love and trust. This is why most of our homes are adorned with photos on the wall. It's a custom that dates back a thousand years and has to do with the fact that people hung portraits on the wall to show to visitors who their ancestors and loved ones were…Today, we continue this tradition, but more so to show the hearts and faces of the people that are welcome in our homes.

Whether your home is a ranch or colonial, majestic or modest, an apartment or a townhouse, the fact still remains that the hearts that enter its doorway are what truly define it as home.

As I pondered how others have shaped the places I have called home, I began to realize that it is exactly these "others" that made each place home. In fact, I have found that even when I have visited my now grown daughter in her tiny studio apartment in San Francisco, or the larger Brooklyn apartment she now inhabits, I feel completely at home, simply because I am with my daughter. And in my own house, it is when my entire family gathers together within these four walls— from the many states they are now dispersed to—that this house most truly feels like home.

How have the people who live in or visit your home shaped how you view the physical place or places you have called home?

If your definition of home centers on being with someone you love, you will be delighted to read God's scriptural promises to make His home in us. Scripture frequently uses the words "dwell in" and "dwelling" to reflect the idea of God making His home in us and us making our home in Him.

Read these verses below and highlight who each verse says dwells in us:

Guard the good deposit that was entrusted to you—
guard it with the help of the Holy Spirit who lives in us.
2 Timothy 1:14

And in him you too are being built together to become
a dwelling in which God lives by his Spirit.
Ephesians 2:22

I pray that out of his glorious riches he may strengthen
you with power through his Spirit in your inner being, so that
Christ may dwell in your hearts through faith.
Ephesians 3:16-17

Don't you know that you yourselves are God's temple
and that God's Spirit dwells in your midst?
1 Corinthians 3:16

These verses refer to the Father, Son, and Spirit alive and dwelling in us. This is an incredible revelation. I am sure you have heard someone say they were going to the house of the Lord in reference to the church they attend; perhaps you have said this yourself. In this instance, the house of the Lord referred to is a structural brick and mortar kind of building. Yet, as believing Christians who have invited Christ into our hearts, He calls our very beings the home and the house of the Lord.

Underline or circle the words home or house in the verses below.

Jesus replied, "Anyone who loves me will obey my teaching.
My Father will love them, and we will come to them and
make our home with them."
John 14:23

But Christ is faithful as the Son over God's house. And we are his house,
if indeed we hold firmly to our confidence and the hope in which we glory.
Hebrews 3:6

**And not only does Scripture tell us that God dwells in us and that
we are His home, but it also tells us that God is our dwelling place,
our shelter, refuge, and fortress. Underline these words in the
verses below.**

Lord, you have been our dwelling place throughout all generations.
Before the mountains were born or you brought forth the whole world,
from everlasting to everlasting you are God.
Psalm 90:1-2

Whoever dwells in the shelter of the Most High will rest in the
shadow of the Almighty. I will say of the LORD, "He is my refuge
and my fortress, my God, in whom I trust."
Psalm 91:1-2

If the Father, Son, and Spirit make their home in us and at the same time, our
Triune God is also our dwelling place, then no matter where our physical body is,
we can feel truly and completely at home.

11.5: Focus on Home

Homecomings on earth are fraught with joys and complications. Many a cinema
comedy and drama relate this human truth with humor and poignancy. In
the years of Jesus' ministry, we never read about Him going home to a cozy,
welcoming, earthly dwelling. In fact, Scripture tells us that his hometown
homecoming was the exact opposite of welcoming.

> Jesus left there and went to his hometown, accompanied by his disciples.
> When the Sabbath came, he began to teach in the synagogue, and many
> who heard him were amazed. "Where did this man get these things?"
> they asked. "What's this wisdom that has been given him? What are these
> remarkable miracles he is performing? Isn't this the carpenter? Isn't this
> Mary's son and the brother of James, Joseph, Judas and Simon? Aren't
> his sisters here with us?" And they took offense at him.
>
> **Mark 6:1-3**

Just after the passage above, we read that Jesus gave these instructions to His disciples:

> Take nothing for the journey except a staff—no bread, no bag, no money
> in your belts. Wear sandals but not an extra shirt. Whenever you enter
> a house, stay there until you leave that town. And if any place will not
> welcome you or listen to you, leave that place and shake the dust off your
> feet as a testimony against them.
>
> **Mark 6:8-11**

What did the apostles do with this advice? "They went out and preached that people should repent. They drove out many demons and anointed many sick people with oil and healed them" (Mark 6:12-13).

Scripture makes it clear that Jesus' goal was not to find an earthly place to call home and stay there. He did not ask us to build Him a beautiful home here on earth. Jesus' goal was to bring the good news about our real heavenly home to the entire world.

All throughout biblical history, places to worship God have been established. God even directed several of the locations and buildings of His places of worship. These physical locations and manifestations of His presence were given to us as memorial signs that He is indeed with us. We are a people who need signs. We wear hats, T-shirts, and bumper stickers to identify us as believing in or belonging to something. God knows His people and He has been giving us signs that He is our God and we are His people since the beginning of time. Yet, God's presence is not limited to any one manifestation or location.

When Stephen was accused of blasphemy and questioned by the high priest, he spoke these words as part of his testimony:

> Our ancestors had the tabernacle of the covenant law with them in
> the wilderness. It had been made as God directed Moses, according
> to the pattern he had seen. After receiving the tabernacle, our ancestors
> under Joshua brought it with them when they took the land from the
> nations God drove out before them. It remained in the land until the time
> of David, who enjoyed God's favor and asked that he might provide a
> dwelling place for the God of Jacob. But it was Solomon who built a house
> for him. However, the Most High does not live in houses made by human
> hands. As the prophet [Isaiah] says: "Heaven is my throne, and the earth is
> my footstool. What kind of house will you build for me? says the Lord.
> Or where will my resting place be?"
>
> **Acts 7:44-49**

Jesus, knowing His Father completely and following His Father's lead completely, did not establish a retreat, temple, palace, or earthly monument of any kind. He came to invite us to come home, through Him, to a thoroughly trusting relationship with God. And He commissioned us to spend our lives inviting other people to come home.

I have lived in many cities and countries in my lifetime and therefore in many physical structures all of which I have called home. One of my favorites was a place I called home for just a few weeks—a home on wheels. When I was a young girl, my parents planned a two-week motor home trip from Iowa to Maryland with me and my six siblings. I loved this vacation and had great fun experiencing this mobile camper as my temporary home.

As I recall this adventure now, the whole idea of taking your home with you wherever you wander is deeply appealing to me. It has become even more appealing as I have come to have a deeper understanding of the Word, because this is exactly what God invites and empowers us to do—to be at home with Him wherever we are. He is our mobile home and we are His. We can be with Him, and He with us, wherever we travel.

Home then is an active place, we might even think of it as a verb. We might consider the daily commission from Christ to be one of "homing"—bringing the message home to ourselves and others, feeling at home in every place and situation we find ourselves, and making people feel at home around us.

What might it mean to you to be actively "homing"? Write your reflections below.

> *Home is the place we bring to everyone, everywhere, when we bring them Jesus.*

Because He dwells in us and we dwell in Him, we are always at home. He has invited us to participate with Him in being home and bringing others home. So maybe our definition of "home" might read like this: "Home is the place we bring to everyone, everywhere, when we bring them Jesus." Or more concisely, "home is Jesus." When we are speaking to and about Him, doing as and for Him, listening through Him, we are home, and we are inviting others home.

There are countless movies about trying to get home, trying to bring someone home, trying to find a home. From stories about orphans, like *Annie,* to stories about those who were lost or left behind, like *Homeward Bound, E.T.,* and the classic *The Wizard of Oz.* The idea of being home is such a basic human longing. There are countless books and feature films that speak to this longing. The four mentioned above have been staples in my home, from my childhood, to young adulthood, and even today, I enjoy sharing these with my family.

Art, especially art that becomes a cultural staple, does so because it touches something inside us. These stories, with their focus on home as a place we long to reach, grab our attention. For the duration of each movie, the lead characters are singularly focused on the one goal of getting home. Let's look at a brief synopsis of each film.

The Wizard of Oz was originally a novel called *The Wonderful Wizard of Oz* published in 1900. This story was made a feature film in 1939 and reintroduced in 1956 as a television movie, becoming an annual tradition and one of the most well-known films in cinema history. Audiences of all ages have enjoyed this film, and I imagine it is because we all relate to the deep desire to get home when we find ourselves in foreign or frightening territory. Dorothy finds herself alone in the house during a twister. She is knocked unconscious by flying debris and finds herself lost in a strange land far from home. After much calamity and heroics Dorothy is told she has always possessed the means to get home. She is instructed to click her heels together and say over and over, "There is no place like home; there is no place like home." She does indeed find herself back home, and once there, she says the lesson she learned was, "If I ever go looking for my heart's desire again, I'll look no further than my own backyard, because if it is not there, I never really lost it in the first place."

Homeward Bound was adapted from a bestselling novel by Sheila Burnford published in 1961. The first film in 1963 was called *The Incredible Journey*. The remake was in 1993, and the Homeward Bound II sequel came out in 1996. In Homeward Bound, a family leaves their pets in the care of a friend while they move to the city for the father's temporary work assignment. The animals mistakenly believe they have been abandoned by their family. They band together, overcoming obstacle after obstacle, to get home.

The movie *Annie* was based on a 1924 comic strip called *Little Orphan Annie* by Harold Gray. In 1977, the comic strip was adapted into a Broadway production, and in 1982, it was made into a feature film. Disney did a TV adaptation of the movie in 1999, and Hollywood released an updated version of this classic in 2014. Annie lives in an orphanage and longs for a family of her own. One critic writes, "In Annie, "Tomorrow" is not sung by an ignorant, stupid, or naive child, but one who's aware of how miserable things can get and how cruel the wheels of fate can be, yet squares her shoulders against whatever life might throw at her, and continues to dream of, and pursue, a better future." Annie is eventually adopted and brings as much joy to her new family as they bring to her.

E.T. was released in 1982 and again in 1985 and in 2002 with new footage added. This film was the highest grossing film of its time and remained the number one grossing film for 11 years. It tells the story of the friendship formed between an extraterrestrial who longs to get home and a young boy whose recently divorced mother is trying to make a new home for her children. In helping E.T. get home, this broken family finds themselves knit back together.

Perhaps you have a favorite movie centering on the idea of home. If so, jot down the name of the movie below and a few notes about its plot.

Perhaps the movie you wrote about shares common ideas with the films I've mentioned. Four important threads in particular stand out to me: (1) The desire to get home, (2) A focus on getting home despite all obstacles, (3) A tenacious hold on hope for a better tomorrow, (4) People who assist the home-goers, despite peril to themselves, and find that they too find their truer homes.

Let's examine each of these threads in the light of Scripture.

(1) The Desire to Get Home

As Christians, we put our hands together and say over and over there is no Savior like Jesus. But once you have found Jesus, have you learned that to find your heart's desire, you need look no further than Jesus?

God gives us this assurance in Psalm 37:4: "Take delight in the Lord, and he will give you the desires of your heart."

As you reflect on your journey toward home, does getting to Jesus direct your every decision, every action, and every word?

We can be like David, the man after God's own heart and declare with him as he wrote in Psalm 27:4: "One thing I ask from the Lord, this only do I seek: that I may dwell in the house of the Lord all the days of my life, to gaze upon the beauty of the Lord and to seek him in His temple."

(2) A Focus on Getting Home Despite All Obstacles

When thoughts of being abandoned by God tempt you to reject Him, do you band together with other Christians, despite the imperfections of God's church, in order to find your way home? Do you turn to the Holy Spirit with whom He gifted you? Are you focused through every detour, challenge, and distraction on getting home to Jesus?

Paul's letter to Timothy, his dearly loved spiritual son, gives us this wise counsel: "The Lord will rescue me from every evil attack and will bring me safely to His heavenly kingdom. To him be glory for ever and ever. Amen" (2 Timothy 4:18).

Psalm 73:21-28 says:

> When my heart was grieved and my spirit embittered, I was senseless and ignorant; I was a brute beast before you. Yet I am always with you; you hold me by my right hand. You guide me with your counsel, and afterward you will take me into glory. Whom have I in heaven but you? And earth has nothing I desire besides you. My flesh and my heart may fail, but God is the strength of my heart and my portion forever. Those who are far from you will perish; you destroy all who are unfaithful to you. But as for me, it is good to be near God. I have made the Sovereign LORD my refuge; I will tell of all your deeds.

(3) A Tenacious Hold on Hope for a Better Tomorrow

In the face of how cruel, difficult, or unfair your life may seem, do you cling to Jesus as your one true hope and source of every tomorrow?

Psalm 91:3-4 tells us: "Surely he will save you from the fowler's snare and from the deadly pestilence. He will cover you with his feathers, and under his wings you will find refuge; his faithfulness will be your shield and rampart." And in John 3:16 we read, "God so loved the world that he gave his one and only Son, that whoever believes in him shall not perish but have eternal life."

(4) People Who Assist the Home-goers Despite Peril to Themselves and Discover They Too Find Their Truer Homes.

When you find people who want to help you get home, do you let them?

Do you value them and still keep your eyes on getting home?

Do you work to help them get home too?

As followers of Christ, God has given us each authority to help and be helped by each other. Matthew 28:18-20 illuminates this concept:

> Then Jesus came to them and said, "All authority in heaven and on earth
> has been given to me. Therefore go and make disciples of all nations,
> baptizing them in the name of the Father and of the Son and of the Holy
> Spirit, and teaching them to obey everything I have commanded you. And
> surely I am with you always, to the very end of the age.
> **Matthew 28:18-20**

Scripture assures us that we have access to all the essentials to enable us to ride the special needs roller coaster as overcomers. By His Word, God sets out these truths as steadfastly reliable: He is with us, He is trustworthy, He gives us a Spirit of courage, He shows us the way, He is our best sounding board, He gives us fellow believers to uplift us, He anoints Jesus as our Savior, He offers a spectacular view through the eyes of the Spirit, He promises joy in Christ, He calls us to rest, and He prepares a home for us the likes of which no man has seen.

Let's commit to trust Him, to activate our God-given spirits, to follow His path, share all of our joys and sorrows with Him, love on His children, process all we experience through the eyes of the Spirit, laugh with Him, seek Him to recharge us, and be at home with Him.

Don't you know that you yourselves are God's temple and that God's Spirit dwells in your midst?
1 Corinthians 3:16

Our home with God is a richer, more ornate, and satisfying place than any home we might design for ourselves. We can be confident in our home with God. Recall 1 Corinthians 3:16 says, "Don't you know that you yourselves are God's temple and that God's Spirit dwells in your midst?" Let's claim this truth and speak the words of Paul as triumphantly as he did in 1 Thessalonians 4:17: "And so we will be with the Lord forever." It is a privilege to be making my way home alongside you.

> So then, just as you received Christ Jesus as Lord, continue to live
> your lives in him, rooted and built up in him, strengthened in the faith
> as you were taught, and overflowing with thankfulness.
> **Colossians 2:6-7**

Home is Jesus and Jesus is home.

Small Group Discussion

Study Eleven - Home Savior Home

After you have individually reviewed the readings and reflection questions, meet with your small group using the suggested format below:

Believe: Our true home is with Jesus.

Scripture Reading: What does this verse mean to you?

> I am the way and the truth and the life.
> No one comes to the Father except through me.
> **John 14:6**

Engage: Review the questions below and allow each person to participate in the discussion.

11.1
- **(1) What are your top five adjectives for the place you now call home? Do these adjectives describe a place of comfort or distress?**
- **(2) What is your definition of the ideal home?**

11.2
- **(3) What aspects of home and home-life give you comfort? If these aspects were removed, how would/does this affect your definition of home as a place of comfort?**
- **(4) What things that you want for your child seem elusive and thus have a negative impact on your sense of happiness?**

11.3
- **(5) How do you feel about the promises given in 2 Peter 3:13 and Revelation 21:1-4?**
- **(6) How does Scripture define our eternal home? (Refer to the reading from 11.3)**

11.4
- **(7) How did you feel about being home alone when you were small, a teen, away at college, or alone temporarily as an adult in your own home?**
- **(8) How have the people who live in or visit your home shaped how you view the physical place you have called home?**

(9) What might it mean, or come to mean, to you to be actively "homing" for Christ?

(10) How can you become more resolute with the truth that to find your heart's desire you need look no further than Jesus?

(11) How can focusing on getting to Jesus direct your every decision, every action, and every word?

(12) When thoughts of being abandoned by God tempt you to reject Him, how can you band together with other Christians, despite the imperfections of God's church, in order to find your way home?

11.5

(13) How can you more effectively turn to the Holy Spirit to guide you?

(14) How can you become more focused through ever detour, challenge, and distraction on getting home to Jesus?

(15) In the face of how cruel, difficult, and unfair your life may seem, how can you more steadfastly cling to Jesus, your one true hope and source of every tomorrow?

(16) When you find people who want to help you get home, how can you more openly let them? How can you show you value them while keeping your eyes on getting home? How can you work to help them get home too?

Celebrate: We are overcome by Your grace, Jesus. You offer us our truest home in You while making Your home in us. With You as the focal point of our journey, we can overcome any obstacle and share the good news of Your salvation with all who will listen. We are never alone, we are always at home in and with You.

Pray: *Lord, thank You for preparing a place for us. Give us the passion to seek You as the desire of our hearts for which we will overcome any obstacle by the power of Your name. Keep us open to those who help us stay focused on You as our goal. Give us the passion to spread Your Word and the hope of our eternal home with all who have ears to listen. You know the tone and tempo of our callings. Help us follow Your lead. In You we have hope for a better tomorrow. Amen.*

(Add prayers, insights, and praise of group members.)

In Jesus is all wisdom,

understanding and knowledge.

By wisdom a house is built,
And through understanding it is established;
And through knowledge the rooms are filled
with rare and beautiful treasures.
Proverbs 24:3-4

Then you will have minds confident and at rest,
focused on Christ, God's great mystery.
All the richest treasures of wisdom and knowledge
are embedded in that mystery and nowhere else.
Colossians 2:2-3 (MSG)

Home is Jesus and Jesus is home.